52 Cups of Coffee

Inspiring and insightful stories for navigating
life's uncertainties

Megan Gebhart

D0189192

IRL

PRESS

Dedicated to my parents,

for trusting me to talk to strangers.

TABLE OF CONTENTS

INTRODUCTION

Who you are in five years depends on the people you meet and the books you read.

I stumbled upon this quote in 2010, and it stopped me in my tracks. I was about to be a senior at Michigan State University and could easily see how my friends and mentors had helped shape the person I had become.

There was one person in particular who showed me the power of meeting new people. He was a student named Brett Kopf who shared an academic advisor with me and was equally passionate about entrepreneurship. The advisor recognized how similar we were and had a hunch we would be great friends. He gave Brett my email address and suggested we meet.

When Brett sent me an email a few days later with an invitation to coffee, I agreed without thinking much of it. I liked meeting new people, and it was just a cup of coffee. I would never have guessed that simple cup of coffee would be the start of an incredible friendship—a life-changing friendship. Together, Brett and I would start a club for entrepreneurs that would become the cornerstone of my college experience and lead to friendships and opportunities that still affect me today.

One day, curiosity got the best of me: *If one new connection could have such an impact on my life, what would a year of new connections do?*

Knowing there was only one way to find out, I decided to embark on an experiment in caffeine and conversation. Each week for one year, I would have coffee with someone I wouldn't normally meet and write about his or her story online at 52cups.com. With graduation approaching, and uncertainty around what I should do after college, it seemed like a great time to ask others for advice.

The intention for 52 Cups of Coffee started out small. I was going to seek out people just outside my network—people I met through friends of friends, social media, or stumbled upon serendipitously. I would meet people in and around Michigan State University, where I went to school, and Wyoming, where my family lived.

As the project progressed, something amazing and unexpected happened. Both friends and strangers began connecting me with fascinating individuals around the world.

I talked to well-known thought leaders, best-selling authors, an NCAA basketball coach, and famous entrepreneurs. The project wasn't just about talking to people of prestige; some of my best conversations came from the most unexpected places: a first grader, a grandma, a WWII survivor and dairy farmer. Rich and poor, old and young, famous and not so famous—each week of the project brought something unexpected and valuable. The stories helped me navigate the unsettling transition from college to real life and develop a stronger platform for living.

Through my conversations, I heard the same advice time and time again: travel while you're young. I decided to heed the advice and put my post-college job search on the back burner and live off my savings while traveling through Europe for five weeks. That decision ultimately led to fourteen months of nomadic living. By the time the project ended, I had sipped coffee in twenty-nine cities across seven countries.

* * *

52 Cups is a journey of serendipity, connection, empathy, and adventure—a story about being courageous, vulnerable, compassionate, and curious.

It's also about searching for answers when you're stuck and not sure what your future should hold. As it turns out, when you start asking questions, you find answers for which you didn't know you were looking.

I wrote this book so that you could read it the way you like—you can read it cover to cover experiencing my adventure, or you can jump ahead to the conversations that most compel you. It is a journey, so you'll notice that the Cups change as I learn, grow, and practice telling other people's stories.

My experiment ended in December of 2011, but the stories and connections have stayed with me. I continue to receive emails from readers who found the project online and felt inspired to start similar projects of their own. And, while I hope you read and enjoy these stories, my deepest wish is that these stories inspire you to take courageous action to build new connections of your own.

Because who you are in five years depends on it.

Megan Gebhart
July 9, 2014

PAT CRAWFORD

Bailey Scholars Room at Michigan State University
Small brewed coffee

Never be afraid to say hello.

My original intention was to start this project in April but decided to wait until July to begin for a multitude of reasons. Finals week was fast-approaching; I was preparing for a six-week trip to Europe as a study abroad program assistant; and, after a full year of classes, lectures, assignments, papers, and exams, my brain was about as useful as a toaster in the middle of the ocean.

July seemed like the perfect starting date, so I marked it on my calendar, put the idea on a cluttered shelf in my brain, and said bon voyage to America. After enjoying good food and fine wine during my abroad program in Paris, Barcelona, and Italy (and after a few weeks recovering), I felt refreshed and ready for this crazy adventure to start. Or so I thought. After writing the initial blog post, reality sunk in: *I actually have to email someone and plan a coffee date.*

Of course, that thought had crossed my mind during the planning process, but there is a big gap between thinking about something and doing it. Like crossing a rickety old rope bridge strung across a canyon: it was scary, but I had to take the first step. It was time to leave the solid ground of the thinking side—and head in the direction of doing.

Fortunately, a great opportunity presented itself that made the first step a little easier. I was a member of the Bailey Scholars Program at Michigan State University working on a Specialization in Connected Learning. It's a small program and very close community of students. The current program director was preparing to leave in the fall to pursue a Ph.D. The replacement director, Dr. Pat Crawford, had started coming into the office to learn the ropes for a seamless transition in leadership.

I had been hanging out in the office (commonly referred to as the Baily space) when I met Pat for the first time. As I was frequently in the Bailey space, I knew over the course of the upcoming school year I would slowly get to know the new director, but it occurred to me that she would be the perfect start to my project. Why not invite her to coffee, get to know her sooner rather than later, and offer her a warm welcome to her new position?

That's exactly what happened. A few days later, we met in the Bailey space, enjoyed a cup of coffee from the Bailey coffee maker (a frequent lifesaver for me), and got to know each other.

We talked about our backgrounds, the number of siblings we had, where we'd grown up, what we did for fun, our mutual love for dogs, and a host of other topics that moved us from strangers to acquaintances. Thanks to the meeting, the next time we would see each other in the space, we wouldn't just exchange polite hellos. Instead, I could ask how her two labs were doing, or give her an update on one of my projects. I would also be a familiar face to answer one of the hundreds of questions she'd likely have as she got to know her way around the community in the upcoming months.

Change is never easy. When the current director finally departed, he would leave big shoes to fill, and the atmosphere of the community would be decidedly different, but after having coffee with Pat, I wasn't as nervous about the transition. I had made a new friend, and now had a better idea of what to expect from the new director.

I decided my first Cup had been successful. I had taken the first major step of this project and enjoyed a pleasant conversation in the process.

I learned three lessons from Cup 1: get to know the people involved in the things you do; be a friendly face for those who are new in your community; and, most importantly, taking the first step is tough, but it's worth it.

Rita Meyer

Starbucks in Cheyenne, Wyoming
Grande brewed coffee

Take life one step at a time, building on small
successes along the way.

Every year, during the last full week in July, I head to Cheyenne Frontier Days in Cheyenne, Wyoming. The self-proclaimed "Daddy of 'em All" is a weeklong rodeo and destination point for my high-school friends to reconnect after a semester away at various colleges. Cheyenne is also where my grandmother and a few aunts and uncles live.

Shortly before leaving for Cheyenne, I enlisted my Aunt Peg to help me find someone to share a cup of coffee. She knew the perfect person: Rita Meyer, a former Colonel in the Wyoming Air National Guard, the current State Auditor and a gubernatorial candidate, attempting to become the first elected female governor of Wyoming. The campaign trail had been keeping Rita busy, but Peg encouraged me to give her a call. As luck would have it, she had a little free time on Saturday. Her warmth radiated through the phone line, and I was looking forward to the meeting as soon as I hung up.

I arrived at Starbucks early on Saturday and made small talk with an old cowboy who had plenty of amusing rodeo stories to share while I waited. When Rita walked in, she greeted me with a big smile, shook my hand and introduced herself. We ordered coffee, found a table out on the patio, and started talking. It didn't take me long to ask the question that was foremost on my mind: Where had she gained the confidence to run for Governor?

Her answer was much simpler than I expected. Rita said she took her life one step at a time, building on her successes along the way. She admitted very openly that ten years before, she hadn't had the confidence to campaign. She needed a career full of large (and small) successes to give her both the experience and confidence that would lead her to the place she was now. But it hadn't just been the successes that helped her. There were failures along the way that were beneficial, too. She smiled as she told me, "You have to fall down and scrape your knees—just hope you don't break a femur!" Confidence is about learning from your mistakes and moving forward.

As you read those words on paper, it seems like obvious advice, and it is, but it is something I won't soon forget. It's one thing to hear those words, but to meet someone who illustrates what happens when you heed the advice is something else. Rita's biography lists one achievement or honor after another. It's intimidating, and if Rita weren't so warm and genuine, she would have been intimidating, too.

However, she hadn't always been so esteemed. This woman had two undergraduate degrees and an MBA in International Business; she had received numerous awards for excellence in leadership during her active duty in the Air National Guard, and had won the 2006 campaign for State Auditor. And yet she was once too shy to talk to people and too poor to take the entrance exams for college. Rita grew up in a small Wyoming town and had to work incredibly hard to become the person she was.

Her impressive resume was not something she built overnight, though; it was a process and a journey. At one point, Rita told me that women need better role models, and I believed her. In less than an hour, she made me realize that who I was that day was vastly different from the person I would be in 30 years—but the change would be the result of small steps. Her advice was that if I worked hard, held onto personal integrity, surrounded myself with good people, and dug deep when things got hard, life would only get better. It was reassuring advice to hear.

Before I left Starbucks, Rita told me that one of two outcomes would occur in her race for Governor: she would win, or she would lose. If she won, she had the opportunity to work hard for the people of Wyoming. If she lost, she would take the experiences from the campaign and move forward. She didn't know if she'd win the race, but she did know that if she didn't run, she could never win—it takes risk to get rewards.

The campaign trail was tough. Rita paraded, did meet-and-greets, drove long hours on the Wyoming roads, made speeches, answered tough questions, and continued to fulfill her duties as the State Auditor of Wyoming. Among all her activity, she had taken an hour out of her Saturday to sit down with me over a cup of coffee and talk. I'm grateful that she did, and I came away with advice I'll carry with me for a long time.

I guess I could say I found a new role model.

AUGUST CRABTREE

Park bench near the fishing lake in Gillette, Wyoming
Tall brewed coffee from Starbucks

Don't let assumptions stop you from great opportunities.

August Crabtree, an unemployed, recovered alcoholic with chronic depression and anxiety, is not exactly someone a mother would recommend her daughter meet for coffee. And yet, that is exactly what happened.

August is a well-known face at the Campbell County Public Library in Gillette, Wyoming, where he has been a loyal patron for many years. He has read an impressive number of books and had just recently started bringing in 4x6 inch prints of photos he'd taken around town to sell to the librarians for two dollars apiece. My mother is one of those librarians and had gotten to know August over the years. She told me he was a straightforward and friendly guy who isn't shy about his difficult past.

August doesn't have a phone, so my mom had to wait until he came into the library to see if he would be interested in speaking with me. He was game, and told her to have me head to the Starbucks downtown, ask for a latte for August and then meet me at the city's fishing-lake park near his beat-up red Toyota pickup. "They'll know what she means," he told her (I later found out it meant an extra-hot, extra-foam latte. I also found out he didn't want to meet at a coffee shop because they won't let him smoke).

As I trekked to the park, I tried to keep my apprehension for the situation in check while circling the lake, looking for a truck that fit his description. My college roommate, Jennifer, who had joined me on my road trip out west, was with me. She was going to catch up on some reading while August and I talked.

As we got out of the car, he yelled in a scratchy and slightly high-pitched voice, "Well you're late! I've been waiting!" Then he let out a friendly laugh to show he was joking. His appearance—cutoff button shirt tucked into ripped jeans; hair pulled back into a small ponytail, and a mouthful of worn-out teeth—caught me off guard, but the nonthreatening laugh put me at ease. I introduced him to Jennifer and handed him the coffee. He asked if I'd brought sugar; I hadn't, and I apologized, but he said not to worry, he'd figured I would forget, so he had brought his own.

He pulled two packets of white sugar out of his pocket and poured them into the cup. Then he searched for something to stir his coffee. His best option was a half-burnt stick of incense from inside his truck; he used it to stir the coffee a few times and tossed it back into the truck. Satisfied with his concoction, he took a sip and let out a startling yelp. Worried he'd burnt himself, I asked if there was something wrong, but he enthusiastically replied, "Nope, it's perfect!"

Before I could suggest finding a place to sit he announced, "I have a skinny ass, and I can't sit down long." I pointed to a bench near the water.

"In that hot sun? I got heat stroke in Arizona and now I can't handle the sun. Let's just sit down right here in the grass." Then he reached into his old truck again, grabbed two seat cushions from the driver's side, threw them in the grass, and took a seat. I had no choice but to follow suit.

I thought I would give him an introduction to myself, explain why I wanted to have coffee, what the purpose of the project was, etc., but I never got a chance. He was telling me stories before I even had time to get situated. My mom had told him that I liked photography, so he handed me his Pentax camera with its long lens, and showed me how to go through the pictures. While I was doing that, he put another packet of sugar into his coffee, this time using the pencil in his front pocket to stir. I asked him a few basic questions, and before I knew it, his story started to unfold.

August, who is 54, spent a lot of time at the library because he loves reading. The habit is the result of his chronic depression. It had started years ago during a time when he began to lose what he called his "zap." It happened slowly, and his workdays started to dwindle until he only had the energy to work an hour a day. Besides sleep, his only activity at the time was reading—sometimes a book a day. He started in the nonfiction section before moving to science fiction, then later to books that explained the human condition—his condition. With the help of proper medication and time, his "zap" had returned for the most part, and the knowledge he had picked up from the countless books stayed with him.

He mentioned alcoholism, so I asked about that. He said he had originally started drinking because it took the edge off his depression: "It stopped me from going crazy and blowing my brains out!" But what had been saving him was also killing him. Just when he would start making decent money and turning his life around, he would drink too much and usually end up back in jail. Things finally reached a breaking point that left no other option than Alcoholics Anonymous. After numerous setbacks, he finally sobered up and has remained sober for 25 years.

At this point in our meeting, August got up without saying anything and walked to his truck for a big Folgers Coffee can. He sat back down, opened the can, and pulled out a cigarette butt. Then he reached into his pocket and pulled out a popsicle stick with a small slit in it and a lighter. I wondered how someone without a job could afford cigarettes; he was about to answer my question. He took a cigarette butt from the can and wedged it into the slit in the popsicle stick, so he could light it and steal the remaining few puffs from the end. During the course of our conversation, he stopped three times to go through this methodical process. Then he jumped back into his story as if he had never stopped.

I asked him how he spent his free time, since he didn't have a job. August said he was trying to find a job—he'd been in construction his whole life and could build anything—and that he spent a lot of time "musing over things." He frequently thought about methods to improve his health, and how he got sick in the first place. He said he now understood the nature of chronic depression, but that wasn't what he attributed his troubles to. He said what made him depressed and prone to drinking in the first place was "not following his bliss." The fear of judgment from his friends and family had stopped him from pursuing his true interests. That lack of passion in his life then created a hollowness that he used alcohol to fill.

* * *

Through all the difficulties of his life—depression, alcoholism, jail, unemployment—and his reading and musing, he came to realize that the path to happiness is following your passion. Passion is what feeds the soul, what fills the hollowness; following bliss is the secret to preventing destructive habits. That is the reason he shows up at the library with photographs; sharing his arts brings him joy.

When August asked me what I was passionate about it caught me off guard. It's a trickier question than it seems, and I couldn't organize the dozens of thoughts floating around my head into a coherent sentence. "I'm not exactly sure," I replied, "I'm still in the process of finding out!" He told me not to worry. "You're young, which means you have the world by the balls. You'll figure it out!" (Note: I left out August's frequent use of the f-word; he clearly has an affinity for using it.)

His simple point resonated with me. In a year I will be diving into the real-world job market, so, between now and then, I better come up with a stronger answer to that question than, "I'm not exactly sure…"

August continually surprised me with his complex and canny statements. The more it happened, the more I realized how I had underestimated him. I would never have guessed he would be giving me detailed accounts of historical events, talking about the sustainability of civilization, or reflecting on the human condition. At one point, he explained the science behind how the mind works, and even drew me a diagram depicting how the subconscious and the body work together and communicate through dreams. He is a man with wisdom to share. Yes, the wisdom might be unconventional; nevertheless, I came away from the experience with a broader perspective of life, hardship, and a reminder that we were all fighting some battle and could benefit from a little compassion.

To be honest, I wouldn't have gone out of my way to talk with someone like August if my mom hadn't suggested it. I'm glad she did. It helped me see that if I judge people based on an outward appearance, and if I only talk to people within my comfort zone, I will miss many valuable—and colorful—conversations.

LAURIE LONSDORF

Grand River Coffee and Chocolate in Lansing, Michigan
Medium brewed coffee

**Decide what you love and find a way to make money
doing it.**

It started with a tweet. Laurie Lonsdorf, a former Michigander turned Washingtonian announced she was moving back to Lansing. Weeks before the move, Laurie decided to get a headstart on meeting people and began connecting with Lansing residents over Twitter. That was how we originally met. We started talking, and I learned that her profile picture, which depicts her wearing a tiara, and her Twitter screen name @PrincessIons, corresponded with her business moniker, the Princess of Persuasion. In Seattle, Laurie had worked as a Self-Employed Marketing Copywriter and Communications Strategist and picked up the princess guise to become memorable and attract clientele.

Marketing was my major and entrepreneurship is what I love, so I was interested in hearing her story. She wanted to get to know another new face, which meant she was a perfect pick for Cup 4. I picked a coffee shop downtown, and when Laurie walked in, I immediately recognized her from her profile picture. We ordered our coffees—she had an iced brewed coffee, while I ordered a regular—and found a spot on the oversized leather couches near the big windows, overlooking the activity of downtown. It didn't take me long to ask the question she'd been getting a lot: "Why did you move back to Michigan?"

Laurie had left for college in Colorado after graduating from high school in East Lansing, and eventually ended up in Seattle, where she'd been for the past 20 years. While she liked the city, she realized it was time for a change. A good friend of hers from high school had been considering moving back to Lansing and was trying to convince Laurie to join her. She still had friends in the area and found the entrepreneurial feel and hospitality of the community appealing, so she decided she would relocate her life back to Lansing.

I was fascinated with her role as the Princess of Persuasion, so I asked what steps she'd taken to get there: did she get a Master's Degree? Where did she find her clients? How did she handle the highs and lows of self-employment?

Her answer, "No, I don't have a Master's Degree, but by now I should have a Ph.D. from the school of Hard Knocks." Laurie had picked up some books and taught herself along the way—she created her business based on trial-and-error. She realized that she couldn't wait around for permission to start a business; she had to take action and hustle. She knew that to stay in business she would have to go out and make a name for herself, so she attended networking events like crazy. That's when she found the tiara and decided to take it to events as a way to break the ice with people. She was right; it got to a point where she'd just walk into a room, and people would call out, "Hi, Princess!"

I stopped her to ask: "How on earth did you find the courage to walk into a room full of business professionals while wearing a tiara?" She said it wasn't easy. From the moment she put the tiara on in her car, to right before she walked into the room, she kept wondering what she was doing. Nevertheless, she pushed through the fear, and the courage to be unique and stand out paid off: her business in Seattle started to grow.

While Laurie had now moved back to Lansing, the "Princess of Persuasion" hadn't quite made the move. She was still deciding whether to rebuild her business in Lansing or look for a J.O.B. (how she referred to any position where her boss was anyone other than herself). She also wasn't sure how the community would respond to a tiara-wearing newbie, so she'd decided to get a feel for the community first.

Plus, there was one other thing stopping her. While she was good at her job of copywriting, it wasn't what she was truly passionate about doing. Laurie loved to get out and talk to people, rather than sit around and write. Her challenge now was to uncover her true passion and then find a way to make money doing it. I was in the same boat. College seniors are often asked what they want to do after graduation; as much as I wished I had a straight answer to give, the truth was that I didn't know. I was still trying to decide what I wanted to be "when I grew up."

I think I was happily naïve in thinking that, once I figure out what I want to do post graduation, I will have my whole life figured out. After talking with Laurie, I realized that the question, *What do I want to do with my life?* never goes away. Circumstances change; opportunities arise. My life is at a crossroads, and there is a high probability that over the next 25 years, I will come to many more. However, what Laurie helped me realize is that while crossroads are stressful, they also create opportunities to shake things up, get a change of scenery, meet new people, and reevaluate what is (and is not) important.

Over the course of our coffee, Laurie's story proved she was willing to take chances, to put herself out there, and to work hard until she succeeded. As long as she packed up those skills and moved them to Michigan with her, she will find a fantastic J.O.B.—or successfully rebuild her freelance business—doing what she loves.

I hope I can do the same.

DAVID MURRAY

Caribou Coffee in Troy, Michigan
Small Pluot green tea

**Live in the moment, have no regrets, and work hard
for the greater good.**

I knew David Murray from the periphery. I had been in the
same room with him on a handful of occasions, and followed
him on Twitter, but we had never talked. I'd first heard about
him when I attended an event he co-chaired in Detroit that
brought together a variety of innovative people to talk technology and re-energize Detroit. Inspired by his efforts to build
a better community, I decided to make time to meet officially.
I was going to be in Detroit for a day, so I emailed him and
set up a meeting.

By one o'clock the afternoon of our meeting, I had already
had more coffee than a girl needs in one day, and David
doesn't drink much coffee, so we both opted for iced tea. So
technically, we did not have a cup of coffee, but we were in a
coffee shop, and I'm making the rules here, so I decided it
counts.

After Cup 4, I'd been mulling over the concept of passion.
*What am I passionate about? How can I create a career around
that passion?* These are the two toughest questions I've yet to
answer since I've been in college—harder than any of the

awful essay questions on final exams I've spent countless hours studying for over the previous three years. I know how to use tests to calculate the mean for statistical research, and I know how to say, "Where is the record store?" in Spanish, but I haven't come across the answer for how to make major life decisions.

I decided to ask David because I knew he understood passion. He voluntarily devoted his time and energy to starting projects in Detroit. Not *rebuild the engine on my old Chevy* projects, but rather, *let's organize a two-day conference on innovation and technology in Michigan* and *bring in big name speakers while we're at it* projects. Undertakings of that magnitude required huge amounts of passion, which meant David likely had an insight or two about the topic.

I found out he had more than just an insight or two. Throughout our conversation, he offered one piece of advice after another and in a straightforward way. In the middle of a response or story he would stop, hit the table for emphasis and say, "Here's something to take away." Then he would explain a concept or habit that had greatly helped him, almost like a thoughtful professor pointing out the points in the lecture that would be on the test. I took mental notes—the test of life is one I want to pass.

Here are a few of the key ones:

Point 1: When it comes to job searching, here's the deal: your resume is not important. Okay, it's important, but it's not that important. What you learned in college does matter, but it's not the deciding factor. You can't let those things define you and the future success of your career. *Decide what you want to do and go do it.* Pick up a book and learn something, ignore the fear that's stopping you, be willing to try something new—those skills will take you farther than a good GPA.

And along the way, pick up "badges" like Girl Scouts: speaking at a conference is a badge; organizing a 5k fundraiser is a badge; completing a research project at your internship is a badge. Failing—if you learn from the experience—can be a badge, too. Then use those badges to show people what you're capable of doing.

Point 2: Build a foundation. David talked a lot about working to improve the greater good. He said he had always tried to make the place he was living better, which led to the second take-away: Decide on the principles you wish to live by. Then let those principles become the foundation for your life—just as concrete is the foundation for a house. A contractor doesn't start building the first floor without a foundation firmly in place; I shouldn't build a career without first knowing my core principles.

Once you've got the foundation, you build life experiences on top of it. My first job in the "real world" will be the first floor of my house, and as I advance through life, I can build upon the previous levels. At one point, I might decide I'm not happy with a level or addition I've built. That's fine; I can renovate, or demolish and rebuild, but the foundation won't change. It is always there, providing support and direction for my life.

Point 3: The final point I'll share is one I've believed for a long time. David said 90% of happiness was surrounding yourself with the right people. David can thrive because the people in his life—from his wife and family to his coworkers and friends—inspire him, support him, and love him. That is

90% of the battle. The remaining 10% is making enough money to put food on the table and a roof over your head, with enough left over to buy the things you need. Combine that with a career based on solid principles that align with your passion and contribute to the greater good, and you will be all right in life.

* * *

If a course in Major Life Decision Making did exist, the hour I spent with David would have made for a great lecture. I realized that it is not about what you do, but how you do it that matters. Our conversation wasn't about how to find a job; it was about how to live your life. I decided that when I begin my post-college career search, I would focus less on job descriptions and company profiles and, instead, focus my attention inward. *What are the core principles in my life? What do I love to do? How can I contribute to the world?* Only then could I look for a career that aligned with those answers. I would build a foundation before the house.

Our conversation also helped me see the career search within the context of the bigger picture. When David receives praise and attention for his efforts, he is quick to point out and praise others who are working equally hard to make a difference. He is not in it for fame and attention—he is in it for the community and the greater good. That is a powerful characteristic to have, and one that resonated from our conversation.

The job or career search can easily become a quest for *me*. Where can *I* make the most money, where can *I* get the best benefits, where can *I* shine? The job market is tough—you have to be looking out for yourself—but David shows the power of turning that mindset around. Yes, it was *my* job, *my* career, and *my* life, but instead of searching for the job or career that creates the biggest impact on *me*, why not find a career where I can have an impact on *others*—where I can contribute to the greater good?

TOM CRAWFORD

Sweetwater Café in Ann Arbor, Michigan
Medium brewed coffee

**Every career path is unique—even if the destination
is the same.**

Two weeks before Cup 6, while sitting with my friend Brett at
a coffee shop, I met Tom Crawford. Brett, who had recently
graduated, was in town for a business meeting with Tom;
Grand Traverse Pie Company had been one of our favorite
places to do homework, so we met there before his meeting to
get some work done.

When Tom arrived, Brett introduced us, and within an
hour, Tom and I had a coffee meeting scheduled for Sweetwater Cafe in Ann Arbor the following Friday. I figured if Brett
liked Tom, I would too.

* * *

The only thing I knew about Tom going into the meeting was
that he was an entrepreneur and loved to travel. Those were
two of my biggest interests, so I knew finding things to talk
about wouldn't be a challenge. When he arrived at the coffee
shop, we ordered our drinks, found a spot in the corner next to
the large picture window, and started talking. I asked him a

few questions, and the resulting answers illustrated the career path he'd traveled down since he left college.

But before I get to that, let me take a quick tangent. Brett was one of my best friends in college (and the inspiration for 52 Cups). The reason was our mutual enthusiasm for entrepreneurship. When we first met, it was clear we shared the same perspective on postgrad plans: we wanted to bypass the 8-5 cubicle life of a corporate ladder-climber and go straight into the world of entrepreneurship where we could follow our passions, create something from nothing and pave new roads.

Fast-forward two years and that is exactly what Brett was trying to do. He had graduated from college the previous December and launched Remind101. He dove into the pool of entrepreneurship headfirst. I, on the other hand, had experienced a temporary change of heart. Living the life of an entrepreneur was still in my line of sight, but I had recently discovered it was not the best move for me right out of college. I knew that I needed to gain other experiences (a job at a company, maybe an MBA) and then ease myself into the pool of entrepreneurship, toes first.

As it turned out, I picked a great person to have coffee with: that's exactly what Tom Crawford did.

* * *

While Tom was earning an undergraduate degree at Kettering University, he worked at the William Beaumont Hospital, which gave him great insight into how a 10,000-employee business runs. He went to work with the hospital after graduation, but eventually left for a company that would help him earn his MBA. While working full-time as a business analyst for a communications company, he was also a full-time student in the University of Michigan's nighttime MBA program. For three years, Tom endured a grueling lifestyle where work and school occupied virtually every spare moment he had.

Once he finished his MBA, Tom landed a job as a consultant for a company called Root, which created the opportunity to travel both nationally and internationally and see how different organizations operate. When his position within the company changed, he had a chance to build a new program from the ground up—essentially becoming an entrepreneur within the comforts of a large company. The program his team created was a big success, but after a few years, the role became routine and Tom moved on to a new company. As he said, "Life is too short to spend doing something you don't enjoy."

His next job was similar in that he had the opportunity to build something from the ground up—but, this time there was a little more risk, and the safety net wasn't quite as big. As his career progressed, he was lucky to work on projects that allowed him to wade into the entrepreneurial pool. These experiences resulted in an opportunity to hang up the corporate suit, set his hours and be his own boss. That's where he is today, as the CEO of Visualization Network—living life as an entrepreneur.

* * *

It is interesting to think back to Tom and Brett's meeting at the coffee shop. It was a meeting between two people doing the same thing—running companies—and yet the paths they had taken to reach that point were completely different: Brett dove headfirst while Tom waded in slowly.

So who made the right choice? And what is the right choice for me?

The truth is that they both made the right choice. Coffee with Tom helped me realize that we each have a career path that is uniquely ours—even if the destinations are the same. The only way to find success is choosing the path that is right for you—not the path others are traveling, or the one your friends and family think you should follow. What worked for Tom wasn't the right fit for Brett, and what worked for Brett probably isn't going to work for me. It is reassuring to know that we are all on own journeys, and as long as I stay true to myself, I will find my right path.

* * *

As our meeting was drawing to a close, Tom asked me if I knew how to get to my next stop. It was my first time in Ann Arbor, and I didn't have a clue, so he borrowed a piece of paper from me and proceeded to draw me a map of where I was, where I wanted to be, and the best way to get there.

As I walked out of the coffee shop to navigate the unfamiliar streets of Ann Arbor by myself, it was nice to know what path someone familiar with the area would follow. It was equally reassuring to know that I was perfectly capable of mapping a successful route on my own.

NOSHIR AMARIA

Espresso Royale in East Lansing, Michigan
Medium brewed coffee

Don't let obstacles and critics deter you from your path.

When my parents dropped me off at school as a freshman, my mom's parting words were, "Now remember, don't talk to strangers!" Of course, she didn't mean it literally (as an out-of-state student, everyone was a stranger to me). It was her way of telling me to be careful and make smart choices.

That being said, I don't think she was too happy to discover I was making friends with strangers on the Internet for coffee.

Noshir Amaria and I had tweeted a few times, just quick 140-character messages about random somethings or others (a common occurrence in the perplexing world of Twitter). Everything I knew about him came from his 140-character biography: *Die-hard Spartan, Athletic Trainer, Future Sports Medicine Osteopathic Physician. Nice guy & friend to all SPARTANS* (Michigan State's mascot). He was a friendly Spartan interested in MSU Athletics—a description that matches each of the 80,000 sports fans who fill Spartan Stadium each Saturday home football game.

So why have Cup 7 with Nosh? Well, when I announced the start of my 52 Cups project on Twitter, he had responded within minutes, expressing interest in being one of the 52. My first reaction was to say okay—the unpredictability of meeting a complete stranger would add to the adventure.

But when the time came to schedule a meeting, I was torn. The truth is, sometimes situations with unknown outcomes make me uncomfortable, and my natural tendency is to avoid them. The rational person inside me kept insisting I go the safe route and ask a friend to recommend someone else for Cup 7. But I had already said yes to Nosh, so I had to hold up my end of the bargain.

At 10 a.m. on a Friday, I found myself sitting across from him at Espresso Royale. After I'd unknowingly walked right past him while he was waiting for me outside (I had no idea what he looked like), he came inside to introduce himself, and we ordered coffee.

I decided to kick off the conversation with the only topic I knew we had in common: interest in MSU Athletics. What I had expected would be a topic to break the ice soon became the focal point of our conversation. He had graduated from MSU with an undergraduate degree in athletic training, worked as a trainer for four years, and was now suffering through medical school in hopes that he could ultimately land his dream job as a sports physician with the Michigan State Athletics department.

Saying that Nosh likes athletic training is an understatement. He glowed when he talked about it, and the conviction in his voice could stop one of the 300-pound offensive tackles he used to tape ankles for before football games. However, achieving a big dream takes much more than just passion, and Nosh was quick to make that point. It takes focus and determination to overcome the obstacles and distractions that undoubtedly get between the dream and the reality. Luckily, Nosh has that too; he'd made up his mind and won't let anyone—or anything—stand in his way.

It had not been easy. Nosh wasn't accepted to medical school the first time he applied. When his second attempt was successful, he was forced to turn down attractive job offers in exchange for the grind of medical school. Some of his professors told him he would never survive school, he failed big exams, and some of his friends listed reason after reason for why he wasn't making the right choice. He even battled his self-doubt during especially difficult times. But, through all of this, he had endured.

He gave some credit to his family. "You have to have people in your life," he told me, "to support you when you can't stand on your own." But ultimately, it had been his burning passion and steadfast resolve to succeed that kept him going: "My mom said that of all the things I've ever learned, how to quit is not one of them." The hard work paid off, as Nosh was preparing to graduate from medical school later that spring.

* * *

I figured my days of receiving advice from athletic trainers ended the day I left the cross-country team to pursue other interests. But there I was at Espresso Royale, learning something far more important than how to get rid of a blister or ease an aching muscle.

Unlike myself and many of my peers who have no idea what we are going to do with our lives, Nosh is still focused like a laser on what he wants to do. He maintains that focus even when the road is difficult. There are easier paths he could have traveled, yet he picked one full of potholes and tight turns. Why? He ignored what his critics said and listened to what his heart told him.

After my cup of coffee with Nosh, I wasn't a single step closer to knowing what my dream career will be; thanks to him, though, I know what it will look like when I find it. Until I can sit in a coffee shop for two hours, glowing with excitement as I talk about what my future holds, I need to keep searching. Nosh is a prime example of what it means to pour your heart into something. We see athletes do this all the time: those iconic moments when players, with all odds stacked against them, go out onto the field or court and give all they have to succeed at what they love. In life, these moments can be hard to find. All too often, the noise of the crowd muffles what our hearts are saying.

I am no exception. I couldn't help but wonder if the reason I couldn't figure out my future is because I didn't have the courage to shut out the well-intentioned noise from people I love and respect and just listen to my heart. Or maybe it was fear of the difficult roads I would have to travel to reach my goals. But the truth is, any path will be full of hardship; that is just the way life goes, and the surest way to overcome those obstacles is to have a burning passion for the dreams that wait on the other side of persistence.

My mom told me not to talk to strangers, but that didn't stop me from sitting down for coffee with one and learning valuable insights. I guess you could say the decision to follow my heart and step outside my comfort zone paid off.

BARBARA BURNHAM

Little Daddy's Family Restaurant outside Detroit, Michigan
Bottomless cup of freshly brewed coffee

Life rarely goes according to plan; just keep growing.

Barbara Burnham's life was right on track: she had graduated from college, found a job, married her college sweetheart, had babies, and achieved her goal of being a stay-at-home mom. For as long as she could remember, that was exactly the life she wanted.

The Barbara I sat down to coffee with at Little Daddy's Family Restaurant outside of Detroit is much more than just a wife and mother. She has become a licensed builder, renovation consultant, designer, and now an emerging entrepreneur with no plans to stop working anytime soon.

The life she has created differs greatly from the life she had planned. What happened? Well, as John Lennon said: *Life is what happens to you when you're busy making other plans.*

Barbara is 5'8" with short blonde hair, wears bronze-colored glasses, and is old enough to be a grandma—because she is one. She told me all this in an email so that I would be able to find her at the restaurant. If she hadn't let me know, I would never have guessed Barbara's age. She has the exuberance and spirit of a woman who is eternally young at heart. I liked her immediately and was grateful our mutual friend suggested we meet.

* * *

We sat down at a table and placed our orders. Then we jumped into the conversation.

Barbara had loved her role as a mother; however, she knew something was missing. Her artistic talents weren't being used, so she found a landscape-design job she could do from home; each night, after she had put the kids to bed, she worked until 2 a.m. completing her assigned project. It was a challenge to juggle, but it gave her the creative outlet she needed.

When her children entered elementary school, she found a job where she could be back home before they came home from school. She worked for a builder who recognized her talents and encouraged her to get her builder's license. She studied for the exam, passed it, and advanced into a new career opportunity.

A few years later, she started doing small renovation projects for friends: kitchens, bathrooms, etc. One day, she had been looking at her finances and realized that when she worked for the contractor she kept only 20% of the profits. But if she worked for herself—doing the same thing—she could keep 100% of the profits. That was when she decided it was time to take the plunge and start a design-consulting firm.

After 13 years in that role, she saw another opportunity. For her sister's 60th birthday, Barbara had made a beautiful piece of artwork out of relief tiles with the logo of her sister's alma mater. The piece, which now hung in her sister's house, received endless compliments from friends. The gift had made Barbara realize the potential for college-themed tiles. With her years of experience working with tiles, she knew she had found a business opportunity that was perfect for her.

The process of becoming an entrepreneur was once again difficult. Barbara had to teach herself new things, take risks, go outside her comfort zone, and deal with the mistakes every entrepreneur experiences at one point or another. Amidst the challenges, the process had come along with big rewards.

As Barbara told me stories of her past, I realized her method: she followed a simple pattern repeatedly. She would make a plan and follow it, but when something felt out of place, or she recognized a new opportunity, Barbara made a change. She stepped out of her comfort zone to try something new. This action caused her to learn, to grow, and ultimately to gain experience and confidence, which she could then leverage into a new opportunity and restructure her plan.

Throughout her life—as in everyone's life, for that matter—she experienced two types of change: internal and external. Barbara's husband had a job that required them to move to places they hadn't planned (external). Barbara realized she needed a job in addition to being a stay-at-home mom (internal). With her mindset, she could cope with both types of change.

* * *

There are two ways to respond to unexpected change: let the change control you, or take control of the change. Barbara chooses the latter. She listens to her heart and works hard in whatever situation life throws her way. As a result, she is now doing a job for which she is passionate and has a wonderful family and fulfilling life. She knows she has much more to accomplish in her career, but she is on the right path. Hers is a constant journey, with no concrete destination.

I greatly appreciated Barbara's insight, because it helped me understand a quote I once heard: *You can do everything, just not at the same time.*

Every time Barbara tries something new, she starts a new chapter in her life. She has been able to do this because she never stops growing and taking risks. She never stays stuck in a rut for too long. Growing, learning, meeting new people, trying new things: those are the things that keep her life exciting and wonderful.

After having a cup of coffee with Barbara, I felt a sense of relief about the future. I learned that, as much as I plan or try to follow a specific path, my life is not going to end up the way I expect. But this uncertainty is okay, because if I react to the change with the right mindset, continually try new things, and seek opportunities I am passionate about, life will be just fine.

WILLIAM WARD

Cosi in East Lansing, Michigan
Grande brewed coffee

Never underestimate the effect you can have on someone.

Lou Anna K. Simon (whom you'll meet in Cup 16) is the president of Michigan State University. She made the above quote to a small group of MSU seniors at a dinner reception I attended a few hours after I had Cup 9 with Dr. William Ward.

The remark was part of a larger talk about the various ways Michigan State was working toward a brighter future. The timing was fitting. Bill (as Dr. Ward has asked me to call him) and I had spent much of our conversation discussing education and brighter futures.

* * *

Bill is a marketing professor, but far from the traditional academic. After finishing college, he went to work in the corporate world before trying a stint as an adjunct professor. He enjoyed the classroom and realized that continuing on the teaching path would require a Ph.D., so he earned a doctorate in Media and Information Studies while continuing to teach in the classroom.

Since earning his Ph.D., Bill had been across the region, working at various universities while keeping one foot in the business world as an independent consultant. One thing I quickly noticed is that Bill is a bit of a renegade—he does things his way.

I could appreciate that because, in my eyes, the education system needs a few renegades to shake things up.

The Internet has changed the game, and the current education system isn't keeping up. The slow change is understandable, considering the size and structure of the long-established university system—it's hard for large bureaucracies to be nimble. Affordable computers, smart phones, and social networks have made access to knowledge inexpensive and easy, while simultaneously increasing the challenge of captivating students' attention. Today's students learn differently than students of 20 years ago, yet most classrooms have stayed the same.

Bill isn't afraid to explore change. The marketing class he teaches at Grand Valley State University doesn't follow the typical protocol: read the textbook, tune into the lecture, and sufficiently memorize the material to answer enough multiple-choice questions to pass the exam. His style forces students to use the new tools of marketing: social media, free online resources, web applications, and expert blogs. His class keeps up-to-date on the latest news, and engages in relevant conversations in the classroom and online—things people actually do in business.

His students aren't always fans of the process. As a teaching assistant at MSU, I noticed students often care more about grades and less about actually learning something. They like classes that are clearly defined, where they know exactly what they're supposed to "learn" and how. Bill's classes are much more fluid, which means they are harder to navigate and require students to be more engaged.

As I talked to Bill, it was encouraging to see someone who didn't let old traditions prevent future growth and change. We often get caught following routines without stopping to check if there's a better way to approach the situation; we fail to realize that the way we've done it before isn't necessarily the best way to do it now.

* * *

I was thinking about this at the reception with President Simon. Michigan State isn't perfect—no university is; education is a complicated and unwieldy endeavor. But, it seemed like the university was working hard to make MSU a better learning environment for everyone. In attendance at the reception were a handful of leaders in the community, and many discussed new initiatives focused on advancing the university, from new energy technologies to more student-centered programs. The energy I sensed matched the energy I felt in Bill; there is something powerful about being around people looking to find new solutions to old problems, to push boundaries.

I think this is a part of what President Simon meant when she talked about the influence you could have on others. When you surround yourself with the right people, the result can be very powerful; even small interactions led to big results.

Even if most of them didn't pan out, what if just one of the ideas presented at President Simon's reception ended up being the spark that ignited change at MSU? Likewise, Bill chose to challenge the norms of education in a single class-room, with just a handful of students he was directly responsible for. But, what if just one of those students learned something about business that made the difference between success and giving up?

That's the sort of effect we can have on people.

JENNY BEORKREM

Beans and Bagels in Chicago, Illinois
Medium brewed coffee

Opportunities are only opportunities if you take advantage of them.

Two summers ago, when I was living in San Francisco for an internship, I came across a poster that mapped the city by its neighborhoods, with each section represented typographically. It had a slightly offbeat but sleek design, unlike anything I'd seen before. It was also my favorite color, and I instantly loved it.

I wasn't able to find out the name of the company that made the poster, but with the magic of a well-crafted Google-search, I later discovered the map I had fallen in love with was an Ork Poster. San Francisco was just one of many city maps they offered. I put the poster on my wish list, gave my room-mate one for her birthday, and told every friend who lived in a city to buy one. I was an unabashed fan.

I would never have imagined that a year later I would be sitting in a coffee shop near the Montrose train stop in Chicago enjoying Cup 10 with the founder and designer of Ork Posters, Jenny Beorkrem.

When I first found Ork, I assumed it was a relatively large company, filled with people working in cubicles and having weekly staff meetings. That perception changed the day I received the San Francisco poster for my birthday. Within the package was a small user's guide, with a note on the back that read:

By purchasing this poster, you've helped a Chicago-based graphic designer live the dream of being her own boss and doing what she loves. From the very bottom of my heart, thank you!

Ork wasn't some big company—it was just one person with a knack for design and a dream. A girl who saw an opportunity, took a risk and changed her life.

* * *

In 2007, Jenny was working a 9-to-5 job as a designer for a company in Chicago. She wanted a map of the city, but couldn't find one that matched her style. So, being a graphic designer, she decided to create her own: the original Ork poster. Friends loved it and convinced her to print a few to sell on Etsy, an online store where artists can sell goods. It didn't take long for the posters to become an Internet hit and for Jenny to realize she had found a way to leave the mundane cubicle life.

Three years later, Jenny was selling 15 variations of Ork Posters online and in a few dozen stores across the nation, she had celebrities and respected designers collecting her work, and she was receiving countless thank-you letters from customers. In short, her simple idea had become a huge success.

Not only did Jenny make brilliant posters, she had found a way to turn her passion into a career. Naturally, she was someone I wanted to meet. I figured the odds of meeting her were small, but I kept the thought tucked in the back of my mind. While I was preparing for a quick trip to Chicago for a conference, I remembered that Jenny lived in Chicago. I didn't have any plans for Thursday afternoon in the Windy City, so I figured, what the heck, I'd see if Jenny would have coffee with me. What did I have to lose? The worst that could happen was she ignored my email or said no outright. I could live with those outcomes, so I shot her an email.

An hour later, she responded and agreed to a meeting. It was surreal how easy the whole thing was: I found her contact info online, sent an email, and the next thing I knew, I had a meeting planned with one of my favorite designers.

The Ork story that's posted online makes it sound like Jenny was just a girl that stumbled upon a good idea. After talking with her, though, it was clear that it had taken hard work, courage, and resourcefulness to turn that good idea into a thriving company. Jenny could have let the fear of hard work keep her from capitalizing on her opportunity. The Chicago map hanging on her wall could have been the only Ork Poster in existence. Instead, she took a risk and now Ork posters hang on walls across the country.

* * *

For my part, I could have assumed Jenny would just reject my email, and thus never have bothered to send it. I could have come up with 100 reasons why I shouldn't have tried. But I had taken a chance, and, as a result I, had a great conversation with someone who was doing big things with her opportunities. The reward was well worth the risk.

That's what Cup 10 taught me: so many times, we miss great things because we are afraid of the opportunity—afraid to try something new, afraid to fail, afraid of the work it will take and the sacrifice required. Sometimes we're even afraid of succeeding. Opportunity knocks, but we don't always answer the door.

I've always loved to sit at my desk and enjoy the map of San Francisco on my wall, but after meeting Jenny I look at it with a new appreciation. It is a reminder that when I see an opportunity to do something I love, I shouldn't be afraid to take a risk and give it a try.

Lisa Gnass

Soup Spoon Café in Lansing, Michigan
Several cups of freshly brewed coffee

Create your own definition of success.

We were sitting at the Soup Spoon Café in Lansing when Lisa Gnass told me a parable:

One morning, an American businessman was sitting on the pier of a little coastal town when a small boat docked alongside him. Inside was an old man with four large fish. The American, clearly impressed with the fisherman, asked why the fisherman stopped fishing so early when he was clearly having a successful day.

The fisherman replied, "I have caught all that I need to provide sustenance for my family. Now I can go home and enjoy lunch with my beautiful wife, relax with a good book this afternoon, and tonight I will go play guitar and sip wine with good friends."

The businessman was astounded at the response and thought—*This man is not living up to his full potential!* So he said to the angler, "You are talented! If you fished longer, you could catch enough fish to buy a bigger boat!"

To which the fisherman asked, "And then what?"

"Well, once you had a bigger boat, you could catch enough to hire men to help you catch even more fish. Then you could buy more boats and hire more men."

Again, the fisherman asked, "And then what?"

The businessman replied, "Then you would have a fleet and large profits, so when you were ready, you could sell your business and amass a small fortune. You would have become very successful and could retire nicely."

"What would I do once I retire?"

The businessman answered proudly, "That's the best part! You'll have enough money to spend your days relaxing by the water, having lunch with your beautiful wife, reading in the afternoon, and playing your guitar at night!"

* * *

Lisa was making the point that all too often, we get caught up in chasing a very narrow ideal of success and, in the process, forget the reason we're chasing success in the first place. Instead of climbing the corporate ladder to achieve the lifestyle we want, we live the lifestyle of ladder climbing, in hopes that happiness will be waiting at the top.

Lisa wasn't immune to this lifestyle. When she left college, she started climbing. She was smart, ambitious, talented, and naturally competitive person. She wanted to prove herself and create an ideal life, so she followed the steps and landed a respectable job at a government agency. Each morning she put on her suit, arrived on time, punched in, and worked her eight hours before the boss let her leave.

Then she woke up the next morning to do it again.

After working weeks without being late or asking for a day off, Lisa asked her boss if she could come in an hour late the following day, so she could go to the courthouse and sign her marriage license. Her boss, shocked that she had the audacity to make such a request, replied, "Your life should revolve around your job—not the other way around."

That's when she realized her job was not a place she was going to thrive.

So she made a change. During her time with the agency, she realized she had a talent for writing and marketing, so she worked out a situation where she could do contract work with the organization instead of being employed full-time. She found more clients and started consulting independently.

The job fit her lifestyle. It also allowed her to help her husband, Cameron, who was running a creative studio. They had student loans to pay back, but they lived within their means and worked hard as they each grew their businesses. Eight years and three kids later, Lisa returned to organizational life as the Executive Director of the Mid-Michigan Ronald McDonald House. She hadn't been looking for a way back into the corporate world. She had been a volunteer on the organization's board, and when they couldn't find a director, she stepped up for the position, but only because it was a cause that was worthy of her putting on a suit again.

That's what I liked about Lisa. She doesn't spend too much time worrying about what others think about her. She already has three wonderful children, a great husband, a meaningful career, and a list of hobbies she enjoys. Like the fisherman, Lisa found the things that matter to her, and that's where she has invested her time.

* * *

As I listened to Lisa tell her story, I started to question my own motivations. In some ways, I understood where she was coming from: I have always prioritized experiences over material goods. I would much rather spend $300 on a plane ticket to visit a friend than on the hottest new handbag. That being said, when I look into my future, I can't help but picture myself living in a big house; it's an image that's been ingrained into my mind by society. A big house signifies a successful life, and, like any serious college student, I want to succeed.

But Lisa proves that success looks different for everyone. Having coffee with her helped me realize that we have to decide for ourselves what it means to be successful and strive for that vision—not for the version that *others* define. More difficult, we must accept that if our view of success differs from the norm, people will judge us, just as the businessman judged the fisherman.

Cup 11 is a reminder that what others think about my career path shouldn't trump what I trust is the best. Maybe that businessman will understand my motivations, but that's all right—it's not his life.

CHAD BADGERO

Gone Wired Café in East Lansing, Michigan
Small latte

Never let good stop you from great.

A slushie changed Chad Badgero's life. Seriously.

Chad's first job was teaching high school in a small Michigan town. He taught English but loved theatre, so after school, he assisted with the school's drama club. He enjoyed working with the kids, but the director was another story. He was a longtime faculty member who never seemed happy and often yelled at students. Chad could never understand why.

Then the slushie incident happened.

During a heated moment at rehearsal, the drama teacher threw a slushie in the face of a student (yes, just like in Glee). Chad couldn't believe it. And later that night it clicked:

That Drama teacher wanted to be up on that stage performing, not sitting in the audience directing. The loss of a dream had turned him into a bitter old man.

Chad came to a cold realization: *Someday that could be me.* He had fallen in love with the theatre when he was in fifth grade and had been involved in the drama club throughout high school. He knew a degree in that field wasn't practical and so he chose an education degree instead. He had always been interested in education and knew it was a good fit. But he never stayed away from the theatre for long.

In fact, the summer after his senior year of high school, Chad hadn't had much going on, so he decided to direct his first show. He gathered his friends, picked a show, found a venue, built sets, made costumes, and rehearsed tirelessly. They called themselves the Peppermint Creek Players.

Chad quickly found out there was more to directing than he had originally thought, but nonetheless, on opening night there were people in the audience. The play was a success! When summer came to an end, he left for college with the assumption that the show had been a one-time occurrence.

As his freshman year was coming to an end, his friends asked about another summer production, so once again—much to his surprise—he found himself in the director's chair. The summer shows continued throughout Chad's college years, but he considered it a hobby. He had decided to focus on teaching. And he thought he was content with teaching English and helping with the Drama club after school. Yet, after the slushie incident, he couldn't shake the thought from his mind: *Someday that could be me.*

He knew he was happy at his job, but would he still be happy in 20 years? Was he about to settle for a stable job that would turn him into a bitter old man, always regretting not trying his hand at a career in the theatre arts?

A few weeks later, Chad told his boss he was resigning at the end of the year. It was one of the hardest decisions he had ever made.

The reaction from the boss surprised him—but not in the way he expected. He was supportive of Chad's choice and left him with words Chad will never forget: "Never let something good prevent you from something great."

And with that, Chad packed everything he had into a U-Haul and moved to New York City to try his hand at acting. The move wasn't easy, but things started to fall into place. Within two weeks, he found an acting job, one that eventually led him to an Off-Broadway gig. He had taken a leap of faith to follow his dream—and he had succeeded. He should have been singing from the rooftops!

He was at first, but his excitement slowly waned. He loved acting, but he realized to survive in New York, he had to take roles that weren't particularly interesting to him. He missed the power he had had during those summers, when *he* chose the projects that meant something to him. He also missed the Midwest, so he left the glow of his newfound success to move back home and start something new.

He knew it was time to turn The Peppermint Creek *Players* from his college days into the Peppermint Creek *Theatre Company*.

That was in 2002. Eight years later, the company has made a name for itself in Lansing, Michigan, producing three shows annually. What's more, Chad also started the Renegade Theatre Festival, which is a free festival that brings together various college and local theatre groups for a weekend hosting 23 different productions in three days.

I asked Chad if he ever thought about what his life would have been like if the slushie incident hadn't happened. He said he thought about it all the time. Without that wake-up call, he would not have faced the decision to sacrifice a good situation to take a risk on something great.

* * *

Cup 12 with Chad illustrates that important change often requires a wake-up call. We cling to good because it is safe—in a stable situation, we know exactly what to expect. Conversely, the potentially great things ahead of us are intangible, uncertain, and scary.

It is difficult to trust that something better may be out there waiting for us, so we settle for something less. We are afraid to trade stability and contentedness for the hard work and unpredictability that comes with striving for something bigger because, if we fail, we can lose the good, as well as the great.

But Chad proved how the rewards can far outweigh the risks. He trusts his gut and repeatedly takes a stable situation and turns it on its head. As a result, he's created a life that he looks forward to each morning. A life he finds fulfilling.

I know at some point in my life, I will have that proverbial slushie thrown in my face, exposing something missing in my life. When that happens, I hope Chad's story will give me the courage to take a risk and shake things up: to sacrifice good for a chance at great.

DAVE ISBELL

Biggby Coffee in East Lansing, Michigan
Small latte

You can choose humility or be humbled.

In cup 13, I learned about sacrifice. I wasn't planning on it, and I didn't want to, but I did.

This happens a lot with sacrifice. It's not planned. It's not wanted. But it happens, and there's nothing you can do about it.

Or so I thought before I spent an hour drinking coffee with Dave Isbell, who gave me the harrowing news that sacrifice would be an unavoidable part of my life—not exactly news I wanted to hear.

Luckily, his next piece of advice was more optimistic. He told me that while I can't avoid sacrifice, I can be proactive and take control of the sacrifices I make.

He went on to say that sacrifice isn't necessarily a bad thing. The act of consciously choosing sacrifice adds incredible meaning and value to life. I wasn't sure I believed him, but I thought back to one of my clearest experiences with sacrifice, and it made sense.

In my freshman year of high school, I joined the varsity cross-country team; suddenly my life was consumed with running. I woke up at 5:30 am, ran, went to class, ran again, ate dinner, finished my homework, went to sleep, and woke up the next day to do it all again. Every choice I made went through a running filter. If it helped my running, I did it. If it hurt my running, I said no.

It paid off. Our team had a lot of success, and I accomplished many of my running goals, but not without a price: I had to pass up on a lot of high school fun in the process.

As I look back, I wouldn't change anything about high school. Running never felt like a burden stopping me from what I wanted to do. Running gave me a sense of purpose, and that made the trade-offs worthwhile. I was willing to sacrifice the short-term excitement so I could reach my goals.

Dave had a similar story. From the age of 13, he knew that his destiny was to be a rock star, so he worked tirelessly and willingly made sacrifices to get closer to his goal. By the time he was 21, his band was asked to go on tour—the hard work had seemingly paid off.

But then he faced another sacrifice. He declined the tour offer and ended the band. The rock-star life conflicted with his responsibilities as the husband of a young family, and he knew he wasn't mature enough to handle both. So he left the stage and the dream because he knew it was the right thing to do; his family had become his priority.

* * *

Dave's story is a valuable reminder. I understood what it meant to make sacrifices, but somewhere along my college journey, I had forgotten. It was easy to do. I was in college and had the freedom to do what I wanted! I was having the time of my life! I didn't want to think about sacrifice.

Dave sees this often happen: college students feeling invincible and free until graduation day arrives, and then reality sets in. Young graduates go into the world, full of pride and confidence, only to be humbled when the burdens of life catch up to them.

* * *

After leaving the band, Dave did some serious soul-searching that eventually led him to his role as Alumni Career Services Coordinator for Michigan State. The job involves meeting with alumni—usually in their late 40s and 50s—unhappy with their career situations and looking for a change.

Many are the alumni who had spent their lives going through the motions; they went to class, joined a few clubs, and then accepted the best job offer without assessing the direction their life was headed. Why should they have? They had a degree and a job—they were set!

But then a few decades go by and when they already have a mortgage, car payment, and three kids to put through college they realize they aren't happy in their careers. But their financial responsibilities prevent them from leaving their jobs. Staying at the same job becomes a forced sacrifice, a burden, rather than an intentional sacrifice that creates meaning.

Dave works hard to change that. His goal is to help alumni find jobs that are aligned with their interests and values so that their sacrifices became meaningful instead of burdensome.

He shared his experiences with me to encourage me to discover what I was willing to sacrifice now—when I'm young and have fewer responsibilities—instead of 20 years down the road, sitting in his office looking for advice.

Without Dave's prompting, I likely would have ignored the concepts of sacrifice and humility until it was too late. I would have left MSU with my fancy degree and full-time job, expecting the world to give me everything it owed me after my four years of "hard work" in college.

But the world doesn't owe me anything, and if I think otherwise, I may end up falling flat on my face.

As Dave said many times during our conversation, "You can either choose humility or be humbled."

Dave's advice gave my previous Cups a new perspective. He told me, "everybody must make sacrifices; you might as well choose the ones you're willing to make. They should be worth the price you pay."

His advice made me ask myself: *what sacrifices am I willing to make?*

DENISE BUSLEY

Grand Traverse Pie Company in East Lansing, Michigan
Small brewed coffee

Instead of wallowing in the problem; look for a solution.

If you've ever enjoyed the wonders of the pie at Grand Traverse Pie Company in Michigan, thank co-founder Denise Busley.

Her story, however, is even better than the pie. Two years after graduating from Michigan State, Denise Busley found herself in a medical-sales job outside Los Angeles. Between student loans and the high cost of living, it was a constant struggle to make ends meet, and she and her husband Mike couldn't see the light at the end of the tunnel.

She had a sales territory that had been abandoned for six months, and the sales forecasts she was expected to meet seemed impossible. When her sales numbers were meager at the end of the quarter, her manager walked in and warned her—she had 90 days to turn her territory around.

She was distraught and angry. The expectations were unrealistic and unfair.

Then, something happened. Right after that encounter with her manager, Denise attended the company's national sales meeting. During the sessions, they made a big to-do about the sales representative with the highest sales of the year. They gave him a big award and displayed his sales numbers: he was making twice as much in commission as Denise was! What's more, he was also from some sparsely populated "middle-of-nowhere" state.

Suddenly a huge mental barrier disappeared for Denise. She realized she was letting the situation pull her down. If this guy could make that kind of money in his state, there was no reason she couldn't match his numbers in LA, where, as she puts it, she "could trip over ten doctors on my way to work."

It was a light-bulb moment.

After the meeting, she ran (literally) to catch up with the president of the company. "I'm going to be the sales rep of the year next year," she told him. Then (once the adrenalin wore off) she had a moment of panic and wondered what on earth she'd done. True to her word, though, a year later, she was sales rep of the year.

For Denise, the change happened because she shifted her mindset. Instead of thinking, *this isn't fair, my territory was abandoned, there's too much competition*, she accepted that she was in a tough situation and focused on the goal she had decided—very boldly—to achieve. Then she worked her hardest to achieve it.

Denise eventually left that job, but the lesson stayed with her: accept a situation for what it is and change what you have the ability to change.

* * *

Two kids and 15 years later, it looked liked a job relocation was in store for her husband Mike, and neither Denise nor Mike could justify uprooting their kids and moving to a new state when neither of them were in love with their current jobs. During a trip back to Traverse City, they visited a small pie shop and an idea hit: they would leave their jobs and start a small 15-seat pie shop. Grand Traverse Pie Company was born.

* * *

In the past ten years, Grand Traverse Pie Company has expanded to over a dozen locations around Michigan, which has brought Denise great success in a career she never expected. Even better, her job gives her the resources to do what is most important to her: helping others. With the business running strong, Denise stepped away from daily operations at the pie shop to contribute her efforts to a group of people working to bring a Children's Advocacy Center to Traverse City.

Her journey has had its fair share of ups and down, but she is flourishing because she looks for the positive and focuses on doing her best in difficult situations. She approaches life with that same mentality she had when she decided, "I'm going to be the sales rep of the year," instead of believing "this situation is unfair, and I'll never make it."

* * *

A few days after meeting with Denise, I was having a bad day; there was something I just couldn't get off my mind. I spent all day dwelling on the bad situation, and by the end of the day, the negative thoughts had caught up to me.

Then I remembered what Denise had said: "Why label something as good or bad? Why can't we just accept the situation for what it is?"

That's when Denise's words about acceptance sunk in. We often get stuck wallowing in situations we can't control: the weather, genetics, the economy, the past, a bad sales territory—whatever it might be. And we let these situations drag us down. We focus on why it's unfair, or we wish with all our might that we can snap our fingers and solve the problem. Why do we do this?

We do it because acceptance is so damn hard. No one wants to face the reality that life has imperfections. So we default to denial. We either dwell on the problem or push it under the rug and pretend it's not there. But that doesn't work. Refusing to accept situations we cannot change leads to wasting significant emotional and mental energy trying to change a situation over which we have no control. We end up entrenching our thoughts in a negative cycle that starts off ineffective and becomes increasingly destructive.

But, if we can find the strength to push through the emotion and pain necessary to accept reality, we can redirect our focus toward identifying the issues we *can* control. We start looking for solutions instead of wallowing in problems.

The process of acceptance has transformative effects. It is the reason Denise became sales rep of the year, and one of the reasons she and Mike have succeeded in both the restaurant business and in their mission to support their community.

As I sat there in my bad mood, feeling the weight of the world on top of me, I thought about Denise and how one sales meeting had changed her life. I realized then that when life is pushing down on me, I am just wasting energy trying to push back. As hard as it is to let go, the more efficient use of energy is finding a way to move forward.

RUBEN DERDERIAN

Michigan State University Technologies Office
Brewed coffee

**The job you get is important, but it's what you do
once you get there that truly matters.**

Have you ever jumped off a high dive? You start on the
ground and inch your way up the ladder, each rung getting
you closer to the impending moment when you must leave the
safety of the board for the uncertainty of the air and the cool
blue water below. You've been waiting for this moment,
preparing for it, in some ways looking forward to it, but all the
mental preparedness can't mitigate the anticipation of the fall,
and the unexpected outcome the water brings.

It's nerve-racking.

That's what it can feel like figuring out what to do after
college—jumping off the diving board into the waters of real
life.

Rung one: Write a resume.

Rung two: Job fair.

Rung three: Interview.

Rung four: Acceptance letter.

When you reach the top of the ladder, you inch your way
closer to the edge, knowing full well there's no turning back.
It's only a matter of time before commencement rolls around

and you're on the edge of the board. Until then, the fear, excitement, and uncertainty mount.

Senior year is fun, but man, can it be stressful. Fortunately, as Ruben Derderian told me, the anticipation is always worse than the jump. I believe him, because Ruben Derderian has had his fair share of successful dives.

* * *

Over his career of 30-plus years, Ruben has been the President of five companies, Vice President of two, an independent management consultant, and, at present, the Associate Director of Bioeconomics at Michigan State University.

That's an impressive track record.

After receiving a science degree from Michigan State in 1965, and then being wait-listed for the MSU Vet School two years in a row, Ruben and his wife decided to move to Baton Rouge so he could work on a Master's Degree at Louisiana State University.

When sales at his brother's retail store started to falter, Ruben decided to take a semester off and move back to Michigan to help out. While helping his brother get the store back in order (and sold), Ruben started working for a small medical device company, which was a rapidly growing industry at the time. He still fully intended to finish his degree at LSU; the job was just something to do in the meantime.

However, he quickly discovered he was good in his new role. With his strong science background, he started going on calls with the salesmen. His ability to translate the mechanics of the medical device into terms doctors could understand made him a valuable asset. The problem was that he was making the sales, but the salesmen were earning the commissions. When a new sales territory opened up, he asked his boss if he could take it. His boss said no; he wasn't about to invest in an employee who was just going to move back to Louisiana.

That's when Ruben decided it was time to switch plans and fully dive into medical sales. His Master's degree would have to wait.

He stayed with the company for a while before joining a new one, where he became Rookie Salesman of the Year, then Most Improved Salesman the next year, and finally, the company's top salesman in his third year with the firm.

His success led to job promotions and work he enjoyed. That's when he set his sights on the ultimate goal: he saw himself as the CEO of a corporation.

That vision set the tone for his career. He worked his way up through the company, learning as much as possible along the way. When he reached the point where he'd done all he could do within that enterprise, he looked for opportunities outside that corporation that would allow him to inch closer to his larger goal. Then he repeated the process.

The recipe clearly paid off: he achieved his goal of running a company (several of them) and enjoyed the successes along the way. He loves his career so much that he keeps failing each time he tries to retire. He always finds a way to go back to work.

* * *

After telling me the long story of his successful career, Ruben turned the tables and asked me about my plans for the future. I didn't like those tables being turned. Because it's not much fun admitting that I don't have a clue what my next step in life is going to be.

But I told him what I *thought* my plans were, and how he responded was invaluable. He said I'd be just fine in the long run. While it is tough trying to find a job when you don't have one, once you have a job, it isn't too difficult to find a new one—especially if you're building credibility and new skills along the way.

That insight, and his story in general, lifted a big weight off my shoulders. I, like many college students, had gotten caught up in the anticipation. I couldn't shake the mindset that I had to find the *perfect* job. Had to! I mean this was going to be the first step of my career. If I made the wrong choice—if I set out on the wrong foot—I would jeopardize my long-term chances at success! Right?

Wrong. It's not the job that decides your potential; you decide your potential.

Ruben didn't succeed in business because he found the "perfect job," he succeeded because he was determined to keep going until he accomplished what he had set out to achieve. I'd bet a lot of money Ruben would have been successful regardless of where he started.

That's the lesson I learned from Cup 15: The job you get is important, but it's what you do once you get there that truly matters.

The reality is that it's scary jumping off the high dive—and that fear never fully disappears. But talking with Ruben reminded me that I had spent four years in college learning the skills necessary to survive in the waters of the real world.

I know how to swim. I can be excited to jump.

LOU ANNA K. SIMON

Grand Traverse Pie Company in East Lansing, Michigan
Small brewed coffee

Hard work is the currency that buys good fortune.

Michigan State President, Lou Anna K. Simon was a first-generation college graduate.

She married her husband, Dr. Roy Simon, while in graduate school but had never fully dropped her maiden name, Kimsey. She still carries the K in her name (and the lessons learned from her Kimsey years) close to her heart.

The Kimseys didn't have much money. Lou Anna grew up in a blue-collar community in rural Indiana. For a stretch, the family lived with her grandparents to save money; when it was time to go to college she chose Indiana State University because it was close to home and scholarship money made it a viable option.

Now she's at the helm of a University with over 45,000 students, a 5,200-acre campus, and a billion-dollar budget.

That's quite the transformation. But in all of her success, she never forgot her roots.

After hearing the intricate story of her winding ascent through the ranks of Michigan State—a journey that began with a Ph.D. in Administration and Higher Education in 1974, and reached a pinnacle in 2004 when the Board of

Trustees elected her to her current role as President—I asked her one question: What take-away from her career at MSU would she pass on to college students?

Her answer had nothing to do with her career at Michigan State. It had everything to do with her father—a man for whom Lou Anna had unquestionable admiration and respect: "Keep learning."

Her father worked in a power plant. He'd left high school early to fight in WWII and later earned his GED. While he might not have been the best-educated man, he had a brilliant mind and throughout his time at the power plant he had constantly tried to learn more, which often seemed senseless to others. Given his level of education, there was a limit to how high he could advance in the company. He did it anyway, and it paid off.

When the country experienced an energy crisis that led to a rapid increase in power plants, there was a shortage of workers with the skills necessary to help build the plants, and her father now found his expertise in high demand. Suddenly the blue-collar employee with a GED was working alongside engineers.

It was a lesson that stuck with Lou Anna, and she shared his advice, "Become good at things you don't like doing."

Whenever she ran into something challenging, or something she didn't like doing, her father reminded her of the importance of becoming good at things you don't like doing, because some day you might need those skills.

Over 30 years, the university went through a lot of changes. And the same was true about Lou Anna's career. She had started with research, which she loved. About the same time

Edgar Harden became MSU president, the U.S. Government awarded MSU a grant to build a Cyclotron on campus. Before they would hand over the money, the government wanted MSU to pass an Affirmative Action plan. Lou Anna was asked to become the Assistant to the President to gather data necessary to approve the plan; she didn't want to, but she said yes because it was a smart career move. The day she loaded a truck with all the collected data to send to Washington (computers and email weren't around yet), she looked forward to returning to her old job.

But the return didn't last long. Within a week, she was pulled back into a new project. There was the threat of a lawsuit connected to the new Title IX Amendment, and once again, the university knew Lou Anna had the skills to gather the required data.

These projects were not ideal assignments for Lou Anna, but she did them, and she did them well. They were opportunities to add value to her career down the road.

Her advice: "Look at the potential scenarios that can happen and do your best to prepare."

This lesson leads nicely to the final point Lou Anna left me with—the one that hit home.

When Lou Anna had been in college, she never had envisioned she would someday become the president of a major university.

It wasn't because she didn't think she was capable (her father had always said the only person who can define your success is you, and she had taken that lesson—like the others—to heart). To some extent, though, the presidency was a matter of happenstance. One thing led to another, and she suddenly realized that if she were going to continue advancing in her career, the last stop would have to be president.

Lou Anna used the term happenstance a few times. It was fate, chance, a little luck, destiny—whatever you want to call it—that had played a large role in Lou Anna's career, as in any career, for that matter. Her husband could have gotten a job in another state; the Cyclotron funding could have gone to another school; her research could have led elsewhere. Different circumstances would likely have led to a much different outcome.

So she became the president because of good luck? Not exactly. Sure, happenstance played a role, but it was what Lou Anna did with those opportunities that made the difference. She had what I had once heard were the three elements necessary to create your own luck: self-confidence, the ability to take risks, and competence. The lessons from her father taught her how to increase her utility. She could look at the various scenarios life might bring and prepare accordingly: focusing on the skills necessary for the task at hand, but also seeing the big picture and developing the skills for the long run.

Preparation is hard work. But Lou Anna's father instilled the value of hard work, and without that, Lou Anna wouldn't be where she was today.

* * *

There have been many times throughout my college experience where the workload has reached overwhelming levels. Times when I'm so sick of working hard I just want to give up—bury my head in the sand and pretend the world doesn't exist. Shout from the rooftops that I'm finished; someone else can do the work.

At times, I've also gotten caught up in the freedom and fun of college and neglected the details. Letting little things slip by. Taking shortcuts when no one was looking.

That hadn't been the case before college. When I was little, my parents kept me on track. I didn't get to leave the table until I had finished my milk. I had to finish my homework before I could go outside and play. Then, in high school, I would go out for a run every day, whether I wanted to or not, because I knew that if I didn't—if I took a day off, got complacent, or neglected the exercises that were neither fun nor easy—I'd have an angry coach to answer to.

College is about learning to do those difficult things on my own. No coaches, no parents, just the lessons they've taught me about the motivation to succeed and the grit to get the job done. Unfortunately, the commotion of college can cause us to lose sight of those lessons; it can deter our determination. Cup 16 is a reminder: Hard work is the currency that buys good fortune.

To be lucky in life requires doing things that aren't fun, getting better when you're already good, and going the extra mile. These things might not seem worthwhile in the short-term, but they pay off in the end.

In the weeks after I had coffee with Lou Anna, every time I tried to make an excuse not to do something, her advice popped into my head. It was incredibly frustrating—I didn't like the added guilt when I already knew I was procrastinating.

But, I know one day I will look back and appreciate the reminder.

PIOTR PASIK

Grand River Café in East Lansing, Michigan
Medium house coffee

Your limitations only stop you if you let them.

I was waiting at Grand River Café when Piotr (pronounced "Peter") texted me to say he was running a little late, so I waited patiently among the college students immersed in their textbooks and laptops. When he arrived, he came through the front door, and then stopped when he saw the two small steps creating an obstacle between him and the front counter.

I waved and started walking toward him; he acknowledged my gesture as he surveyed the situation. When I got to the door, I said a quick hello, let him know there was a stair-free entrance around the corner, and held the door while he navigated his electric wheelchair out of the small entryway.

He followed me through the other door to the front of the crowded coffee shop. He ordered a large hot chocolate; I went with a regular house coffee. He generously paid for both—straining to reach over his scooter to hand the signed receipt back to the cashier.

When our drinks were ready, I carried both to an empty table. Piotr parked and laboriously maneuvered from his scooter into the chair, taking a moment to get situated before we started our conversation.

If I had been alone, the entire process would have taken two minutes. If Piotr had been alone, it would have taken ten.

Piotr has spastic cerebral palsy—a condition that causes degenerative mobility. He can't get around without his scooter or walker, and when he goes out, it is a slow process. After observing this, I assumed Piotr probably didn't get around much. Ten minutes into the conversation, I realized how wrong my assumption was.

He had recently returned from a 10-day trip to Ireland, a trip he took by himself. What's more, he had done it without much planning. Piotr, who was currently working on a Master's in Disabilities Counseling at Michigan State, had received grant money to attend a conference there. He bought a ticket and planned to work out the finer details once he arrived in Europe. He knew he wanted to catch a soccer game (he's a huge fan) and visit his family in Poland for a few days (he emigrated from Poland when he was 11), so he decided to use the conference as an excuse to go on an adventure.

Within hours of landing, he had navigated the foreign city, found a taxi driver (who graciously volunteered to take him to a scooter-rental store), found his hotel, and made it to the soccer game he'd bought tickets to before leaving the States. His afternoon was spent surrounded by rambunctious soccer fans, watching his favorite sport; this was just the start of what Piotr called "the trip of a lifetime." Of course, he ran into a few challenges during the trip—every traveler does—but the Irish were very accommodating, and he didn't meet any problems he couldn't solve.

I know what it's like to travel internationally, so I was already impressed with Piotr. However, what he said next blew me away. His other passion was intramural soccer—in a league of able-bodied college kids.

It didn't matter that he needed a walker to get around, or that he had clunky movements when he did; he never missed an opportunity to be out on the field. He might stand out among the energetic 20-something college boys sprinting up and down the field as he waited near the goal for an opportunity to score, but he loved every minute.

It began when he needed an elective credit for his undergrad degree (also at MSU). He loved soccer, so that was what he chose. While many of the exercises were beyond his ability, he focused on the drills he could do, and his skills improved. Initially, he was apprehensive about how his classmates would react when he joined the game, but over time—and with the support of his classmates and a small fan club—he became more comfortable.

It had reached a point where you couldn't get him off the field. And while he loved the rush of being out on the field doing something he loved, the real motivation for his efforts wasn't to score goals or win games. He was trying to change perceptions. He wanted to normalize disabilities and help people see that people with disabilities were just regular college students facing unique challenges.

Piotr had an incredible perspective on life and his condition. I asked him how he did it.

He said it hadn't always been easy. For a long time he asked the "why" questions: Why me? Why did this happen? Why can't I be like everyone else?

When he had exhausted all possible questions, he realized that his condition wasn't going to change; he was stuck with cerebral palsy for life, and he needed to accept that. At the same time, he recognized he wasn't the only one asking those questions. As Piotr put it, everyone had something: some obstacle or challenge they had to fight. Some people had visible obstacles, while others were fighting a silent battle; life was an uphill battle for everyone. That was when he decided he wasn't going to let his disability stop him from living an incredible life.

And that was what he was doing. When he saw an opportunity to travel abroad, he took it. He was passionate about soccer, so he signed up. He could have used his condition as an excuse both times, but he didn't.

* * *

This is the lesson from Cup 17: Our limitations only stop us if we let them. You can sit back and wait for the conditions to be perfect—make a hundred excuses why you can't do something—or you can say, "screw it!" and find a way to make it happen.

We all have lists of things we want to do: travel abroad, run a marathon, go to law school, skydive, start a business, learn a new language. And so we say someday we'll get around to doing these. Why not today? Well, I'm too busy; I don't have the money; I have this "thing" that's stopping me.

Those are just excuses we use so we don't have to face the fact we are scared to go outside of our comfort zone where we might fail or face ridicule. We decide that "someday" we'll do it. But the truth is, starting new things never gets easier—in 20 years, there will be whole new set of excuses that prevent us from following our passions. And if our dreams never come true, we can just blame our "thing."

That is, unless we spend an hour with someone like Piotr, after which we realize our thoughts are the only thing holding us back.

He knew it was a cliché to say, but he said if he could achieve his dreams, anyone could. Piotr is a guy with so much stacked against him, and yet he is one of the happiest people I have ever met. He is living an incredible life that he loves.

All because he decided he wasn't going to use his limitations as an excuse. I'd say he made the right choice.

VINCE FOSTER

Starbucks in East Lansing, Michigan
Grande Americano

Surround yourself with good people.

Academic advisors are supposed to provide support for students working toward their goals. That wasn't the case for Vince Foster. It was an advisor, who told him he *couldn't* achieve his goals that motivated his career as an accountant.

During Vince's undergraduate career, accounting was considered the toughest major within the business college. When it came time to declare his major, Vince decided on accounting to challenge himself.

His academic advisor thought otherwise. This was back when the drinking age was 18 and, well, let's just say he had enjoyed his first few semesters of college. The advisor wasn't afraid to tell Vince exactly how he felt. He took one look at his transcript and concluded he didn't have the grades to be accepted, let alone survive the program. That wasn't what Vince wanted to hear. He left the meeting with a silent resolve to prove he could get into the accounting program.

And he did. He was accepted, earned his degree, and took a position in Houston with Arthur Andersen.

* * *

It was amusing to listen as Vince relived his college experi-ence—everyone loves an underdog story—but what had me captivated was the story about how he left Arthur Andersen after 19 years (long before the company dissolved due to legal issues) to start his own venture: Main Street Capital Corpora-tion, an investment firm for small-to-medium sized businesses.

Starting Main Street Capital had been a risky decision. Vince had a wife and three kids relying on his success, in addition to the friends and family who were willing to invest their savings into his company. With so many interests at stake, failure wasn't an option. But, with 20 years of experi-ence and a strong business plan, he had the confidence to make it work.

* * *

12 years later, Vince's company is a success. Main Street Capital now has several dozen employees, manages a portfolio of 40 businesses, and has big growth plans for the future.

I asked him how he had made it successful. Vince told me, "I hire people smarter than me, who are more talented than me." Vince has figured out where his own strengths are and that allows him to identify employees whose strengths balance out his weaknesses. Due to his hiring philosophy, he has surrounded himself with good people.

It's not the first time a group of good people has led to his success. While getting into the business college was a step in the right direction for Vince, the real magic happened when he joined a business fraternity, where he quickly became good friends with many of the members. It was a group of ambitious students who worked hard and still managed to find time for a social life. It was a transformative group for him. He had always had close friends, but there was something powerful about surrounding himself with supportive, motivated, and bright students, all interested in the same topics.

I could relate—in a big way. My transition to college had been relatively easy. I joined the cross-country team, which meant I had a ready-made group of friends the day I started school. I also had two coaches keeping an eye on me (a comforting feeling when 1,000 miles from home). I still had to find my place within that group, but instantly surrounding myself with good people had been a nice way to get college started on the right foot.

I took that support for granted. It wasn't until I left the team and found myself without the support system that I realized how important it had been in my life. I still had great friends on the team, but I no longer had a three-hour block of time I spent with them every day. Suddenly, I felt lonely and entirely unmotivated. The loss of a social network made for a rough sophomore year.

Then, during my junior year of college, I stumbled into a group of students who had a transformative effect on me. It was a much less formal setting than Vince's fraternity; we were just a group of student entrepreneurs getting together once a week to have a beer and talk business. However, before we knew it, the group started to grow. There is something magical about getting a bunch of passionate, like-minded people in one place. And 30 years from now, when I reminisce on my time at Michigan State, it will be this group of people that I talk about.

STEFAN OLANDER

Cafeteria at the Nike Headquarters in Beaverton, Oregon
Medium Americano

Don't work so hard that you stop loving what you do.

I got my first pair of Nike running shoes in eighth grade—back when it was a feat to finish a five-mile run. By my senior year of high school, I had a dozen pairs piled in the corner of my closet, worn from countless miles traveled along the familiar streets of my hometown.

My interest in running continued to grow; in 2008, I took a road trip out to Eugene, Oregon to watch my roommate compete in the Olympic Trials. While there, I bought a book called *Out of Nowhere: The Inside Story of How Nike Marketed the Culture of Running*—a book that chronicled how the company had begun with Bill Bowerman making shoes with a waffle iron in his garage, then grew into a sportswear giant that significantly changed the world of running.

As a runner and marketing major, I had a lot of respect for Nike, which I had mentioned to Bill Ward, Cup 9, while carpooling to a conference in Detroit. He asked me the dreaded question I'd been hearing a lot, "So, what are your plans for after college?"

It was a well-intentioned question I felt I should have had a good answer for, but I didn't, so the question always created stress. I settled on telling Bill that I liked Nike, and he mentioned that his friend Stefan Olander worked on the team that developed the Nike+ running system, and he'd be happy to introduce me. I was heading to the West Coast for Thanksgiving, so the timing was perfect. After a few emails among the three of us, I had a meeting setup with Stefan at the Nike World Headquarters in Oregon.

* * *

The meeting was on the Wednesday before Thanksgiving. It was a frosty morning, and, despite the Nike campus feeling deserted due to many employees being gone for the holiday, the place was as impressive as I had expected. I met Stefan in the Jerry Rice building, and we walked across the street to the cafeteria. Bill had told me Stefan had been born in Sweden, so as we stood in line to order, I asked how long he had been in the United States. "Six years," he said as he began to explain the series of events that had led to his current position. By the time we had our drinks and found a place to sit, I'd learned that the Nike Headquarters hadn't even been Stefan's anticipated destination.

He had originally wanted to be a ski guide in the Alps; after earning a degree in engineering, he hit the slopes, leading tours while working at a ski store on the side. His boss at the shop had taken a job working with a then-young company called Nike and convinced Stefan to follow suit.

After a few years working the Nordic division, and a few courses in marketing, Nike moved Stefan and his family to Holland, to work with brand management for a five-country region. This happened when the Internet was just starting to gain traction, and Nike had one website it used for all of its regions. The strategy hadn't made any sense to Stefan. He understood how Europeans had different tastes than Americans, so he and his team had taken on the task of rolling out customized websites for each region.

Stefan's success with the new technology helped him build a reputation as a leader in digital marketing and landed him his current job in Portland: Vice President of Digital Sports. That included work with Nike+, Ballers Network, and Nike's latest installment of digital awesomeness: Nike Grid in London. It wasn't where he had expected he'd be when he left college, but he had followed his passion and ended up with a job he loved.

Stefan had a laid-back disposition, a healthy perspective on life, interesting background, and clearly a creative mind. I knew his rise through the ranks inevitably taught him a lot, so I asked him what advice he would give the 22-year-old version of himself.

It took him a minute to answer the question. I got the impression he appreciated both the good and bad in life as necessary steps of his journey, and that he didn't have many regrets. But he finally decided on an answer, and I will never forget what he said, "I am certain I could have achieved the same level of success without working so hard."

He explained he had never minded working hard—that's a prerequisite; he was talking about pushing himself and the people working with him *too* hard—like a radio dial turned a few notches past the prime spot. If he could have adjusted the dial to find the right balance of effort, he would have been more focused, more efficient, had more fun, and ended up just as successful.

* * *

The thought echoed in my mind. It's the opposite advice you typically hear, but I knew exactly what he meant.

Preparing for the Nike meeting had me reminiscing on my cross-country days, and as I sat there with Stefan, something clicked: I had had the most success running during times when I was relaxed and having fun. I wasn't having fun *because* I was succeeding; I was succeeding *because* I was having fun. The summer before my high school senior year, my passion for the sport had engulfed me. I had looked forward to daily runs—once willingly leaving an energetic wedding reception to run eight miles in the dark. I loved the pressure of challenging workouts; I counted down the days until big meets. That passion and work led to success.

But as that success escalated, so had the pressure to continue succeeding. Somewhere along the line, the stress had turned my passion into an obligation. Continuing on to a Division I cross-country team in college definitely hadn't reduced the stress. I told myself I *had* to work harder, *had* to hit a certain time at practice, *had* to run more miles.

My ambition had worked against me. Instead of getting better, I got worse.

I quit the team after one year. I said it was because there were other opportunities at Michigan State I wanted to explore—which was true—but the other factor, the one I couldn't admit for a long time, was that I was burned out.

I had done just what Stefan had said he would tell his younger self not to do: I had turned the dial way past the optimal setting. I became so serious about running, I started looking at fun as a distraction I didn't have time for—something that just got in the way of the hard work I had to do.

Stefan showed me that success isn't about working as hard as possible; it's about finding the right balance and having fun along the way.

I should have known from my running experience that I would be more successful if I kept life fun, but it wasn't until I heard it from someone with a career I admired that I believed it.

SAM ROSEN

Lovely Bake Shop in Chicago, Illinois
Regular coffee

There is more than one way to approach life.

Cup 20 came with a riddle:

If I handed you a pen and asked, "what is this?" you would say, "a pen." If I asked what you did with the pen, you would say, "write." And you would be correct because that's what it is, and that's what it does.

But what if I handed the same pen to a dog? She wouldn't use it to write; she would use it as a chew toy. Is she wrong? No, from a dog's perspective, a pen is more useful as a toy than a writing tool.

Hand the pen to an absent-minded college student, and it could become a bookmark. An engineer might see it as a combination of parts: a plastic casing that holds a tube of ink with a dispensing mechanism. You get the picture.

The pen doesn't have to be a pen—it can be whatever you make it.

* * *

The above story was a concept Sam Rosen presented to me after we'd been volleying stories back and forth for 45 minutes inside an adorable café. I was in Chicago visiting a friend who introduced me to Sam. The snow outside was blowing fiercely, but Sam's relaxed demeanor and creative perspective made for easy and enjoyable conversation. I told him a little about myself, and he chronicled the Bohemian steps he had taken that had led to his current role as a founding partner at One Design Company.

At some point in the conversation, he stopped and said there were two ideas by which he lived. The first was a quote by former Major League Baseball player and general manager Branch Rickey: *Luck is the residue of design.*

The second, the pen-parable, was a Buddhist principle about perspective and value; a reminder that there was more than one right way to approach any situation.

Sam had an interesting approach to life, especially school. One of the first things he said to me was that he knew early on he was good at computers—not necessarily the best, but certainly good enough to turn it into a career. The value a traditional education didn't mean much to Sam, he had self-taught skills and knew what he wanted to do with his life. Arbitrary learning didn't seem worth the effort.

That perspective explained the 2.1 GPA on his high-school diploma. In fact, during his last week of high school, he had had to beg one of his teachers to give him a passing grade so he could graduate.

However, it's not that he wasn't capable of getting good grades. Sam had decided he wanted to go to the Art Center College of Design in Pasadena—a leader in art and design education. Unsurprisingly, he didn't get accepted, but he did receive a handwritten rejection letter saying they liked him, but with a 2.1 GPA, they weren't sure he could handle the rigorous academics of the school.

The value of school had now changed for Sam; it became his passport to Pasadena. He spent a semester at Colombia College in Chicago, finished with a strong GPA, and transferred to the Art Center.

He left after a year.

His year at the rigorous school reminded him that, from his perspective, college was just a place where you spent a lot of money so someone could force you to do work and then criticize it when you finished. Sam had been starting projects his whole life; he didn't need to pay someone for that, so he dropped out.

At that point in time, he found work with a web-design firm. The owner, who charged $150 an hour for each project, would contract work to Sam, who worked for $50 an hour. Sam looked at the situation and realized something: if this guy could make $150 an hour and Sam was doing most of the work, there was no way Sam couldn't do the same, or better. So he decided to start a web-design firm.

He figured if his idea failed; he could always go back to working for someone else.

* * *

After six years, it looked like Sam wouldn't need to apply for jobs anytime soon. One Design had seen double-digit growth for the past five years, grown to a dozen employees and established a client list that includes Groupon, Xerox, and New York Magazine.

Sam's approach doesn't work for everyone—in fact; it doesn't work for a lot of people. But Sam is successful because he is both passionate about what he is doing and willing to spend hours developing his skills. Whether knowingly or not, Sam took an honest assessment of himself—his likes and dislikes, strengths and weaknesses—and discovered the path that works best for him. With a supportive family and the courage to take calculated risks, he made his approach work.

* * *

Of course, I'm not advocating a lax approach to school or dropping out of college; I'm pointing out the value of finding what works best for you. Just like there is more than one way to look at a pen, there is more than one way to approach life, school, careers, etc. You have to pick one, and then exert the effort needed to make it work.

That's been a recurring lesson over first 20 Cups. But what is different about Cup 20 is this: Instead of helping me find my approach, Sam reminded me to respect the choices others make. Everybody's approach is different, and just because they don't do things your way doesn't mean they are doing them the wrong way.

I don't want people judging my life's ambitions, so I shouldn't judge theirs. It's easy to discount the kid who barely survived high school and left college early. But one day, that kid could be your boss.

TORYA BLANCHARD

Good Girls Go To Paris Crepes in Detroit, Michigan
Small house coffee

You only get one life—make the most of it.

Torya Blanchard was caught shoplifting a few weeks before a trip to Paris for her 16th birthday. When she got home, her mother's furious words were simple, "Only good girls go to Paris!"

Her mother, who had a change of heart and let Torya go on the trip, doesn't remember the scolding, but it was something Torya would never forget. Fifteen years after that trip to Paris, when Torya decided to open a crepe shop in Downtown Detroit, she knew exactly what to name it—Good Girls Go to Paris Crepes.

* * *

A few months prior to Cup 21, I was at a conference in Detroit, when I overheard a few snippets of a conversation happening next to me, something about a can't-miss crepe shop. When I got back to East Lansing, I did some research and discovered Good Girls and its owner, Torya Blanchard, the "Francophile, fashionista and fearless crepe-maker." With a description like that, I knew I needed to talk to her.

So there I was, sitting in the small shop, with its boldly painted red walls lined with French film posters and a large menu of crepe options that made my mouth water. The woman at the counter told me Torya was on her way, and offered me a cup of coffee. I found a table where I could watch the employees making the crepes, which brought back great memories of my two trips to Paris.

When Torya walked in, her big smile and loud "hello" shook me out of my trip down memory lane. I stood up to introduce myself, reaching to shake her hand. She ignored my gesture, instead giving me a big hug—talking continuously as she grabbed herself a cup of coffee and pulled up a chair at my table.

I didn't know what to expect from the meeting, but I was sure of one thing: it was going to be fun. Torya had a personality that filled the room. It wasn't just her big smile and booming voice, it was also her Ray Ban glasses and hair with a mind of its own. She had a quirky demeanor that mixed a cool composure with contagious enthusiasm that made swapping stories even more entertaining.

* * *

Torya had been working on an engineering degree at Michigan Tech when she decided it was too boring for her tastes. She'd run into a woman at a Study Abroad Fair who told her about an opportunity to work in Paris as an au pair. Torya had loved the idea—a two-year adventure in Paris would give her time to figure out a new direction for life. So she booked her ticket, packed her bags, and took off across the ocean. By the time her trip had ended, she knew what she wanted to do. She transferred to Wayne State University, earned a degree in French and started teaching at a Detroit high school.

Torya enjoyed teaching French. She lined her classroom walls with French film posters and told stories about French culture. She loved getting to know the students, and although the administrative tasks might have been draining at times, she had no plans to leave her job.

Until a seemingly insignificant thing happened.

Torya had left work on a Thursday afternoon to catch a spinning class, but when she got to the gym, the class was empty. She had come on the wrong day. The mix-up bothered her, and she thought, "Really, Torya? Your life is so busy and complex; you can't get to a spinning class on the right day? This is what your life has come to?"

The moment made her notice something she hadn't noticed before. She wasn't as happy with life as she knew she could be. She decided to get on a bike anyways and do some thinking—take an inventory of her life. She asked herself a basic question: *What do I love to do?*

She knew she loved people, and loved French culture, but how could she combine the two? A restaurant? The only thing she knew how to cook was crepes…but her crepes were *good*, and she loved making them.

That's when it clicked—right there on a bike in an empty exercise room, Torya realized what she needed to do. She would leave her teaching job of five years and open a crepe shop.

A few days later, she walked past an empty storefront where a hotdog stand had recently shut down. It was just a small 48-square-foot shop, but to Torya, it was perfect. Her friends and family thought she was crazy, but she didn't care. It was what she now calls her "Fight Club moment"—the instant she decided to go all-in, to risk everything to make the dream a reality. She called the number on the for-sale sign, cashed in her 401k, and got to work.

It took months of planning, long hours, and a lot of elbow grease before the day she had been anxiously awaiting arrived: the day she opened the doors for her first customers.

Between the delicious crepes, Torya's welcoming personality and the support of a tight-knit group of Detroit entrepreneurs, word about Good Girls spread, and her business took off. Within a few months, Good Girls had outgrown the small store-space and upgraded to a larger location.

Torya had traded in the security of a comfortable 9-to-5 life as a teacher, for a job that required late nights, early mornings, and all the mental and physical energy she had, but she wouldn't trade it for the world. Even after the most hectic and exhausting day at the store, she still wakes up the next day excited to go back and do it all again.

* * *

I asked Torya how she had dealt with the inevitable stress of the decision to start Good Girls. She said it had been stressful, but that wasn't going to stop her—the crepe store was something she had to do. "When I get older," she said candidly, "I want to look back and say I did everything I wanted to do."

It is such a simple statement, but a profound reminder that we only live once—we have one shot to make life everything we want it to be. It's an idea that can often be forgotten as we get caught up in the to-do lists of day-to-day life. Torya doesn't forget it. She tries to squeeze the most out of every moment of her life. The result is a girl who is full of life and has a contagious spirit.

When I left Good Girls, my mind was racing with thoughts: *What do I love? What do I want out of life? Am I happy with where I am?*

I couldn't answer all the questions sparked by the conversation with Torya, but Cup 21 made me realize these were questions I had to keep asking until I discovered a dream that was worth risking everything to make happen. That moment might be tomorrow; it might be when I'm 30. Whenever it happens, I will think about Torya's "Fight Club moment" and the courage and determination she had to get the most out of life.

Because if I've only got one shot at life, why wouldn't I do everything possible so that I too can someday look back at my life and say, "I did everything I wanted to do"?

ABBY WARD

Brother's Coffee in Gillette, Wyoming
Small house coffee

Education is the best remedy for ignorance.

Just when you think you know someone, you learn something new. Richard Ward works at the Public Library in Gillette, Wyoming with my mom. As I was growing up, the library was practically my second home, so I've known Richard and his wonderful wife, Rachel Nava, for a long time.

The family member I did not know was Abby, the daughter they adopted from a Lakota Sioux tribe six years before. I had seen pictures, and even held her as a newborn, but I'd left for school in Michigan before she was old enough to know. When I was home for Christmas, I stopped by the library to catch up with Richard and see if he had recommendations for someone to have coffee with—he suggested Abby.

He told me she had a very interesting perspective. Although she was just six years old, she understood that she had been adopted, and was knowledgeable about her Lakota heritage (Rachel was also in the Lakota tribe). He made a good point—and librarians have rarely led me astray—so I agreed and called Rachel to schedule a play-date with Abby.

* * *

A few days later, I found myself waiting at Brother's Coffee, trying to calm my nerves. I'm not typically nervous in meeting new people, but I lived in a college town, which meant my world involved a disproportionate number of 20-somethings. I had forgotten how to relate to the *Dr. Seuss* demographic.

Abby walked in, looking pretty harmless, but I was still nervous and didn't know what to expect. Rachel asked if she should stay or leave the two of us alone to talk; I said whatever she felt more comfortable with was fine with me. She said she would run a few errands and be back. Abby and I said goodbye and walked to the counter for drinks. I ordered a coffee and Abby said, in a barely audible whisper that she'd like a Coke—with a straw.

I started the conversation by covering the basics: what Santa had brought for Christmas, what grade she was in, her favorite subject in school (answers: violin, first, science). She was adorable as she answered my questions, her legs swinging back and forth as she sipped her Coke—the straw fitting perfectly into the space where her front baby tooth had been. I could tell she was growing more comfortable with the situation once her responses grew from a few words to full sentences and she started telling me unprompted stories about recess. I was growing more comfortable too.

When I asked Abby what Indian tribe she belonged to, she said she was a Lakota. I asked her to tell me about some of the fun things she did as a Lakota Sioux. It was fun to hear the excitement in her voice as she told me about Sun Dances and Pow Wows (where she got to learn dances and wear costumes), her trips to visit her tummy (biological) mommy, and playing with her cousins at events like the Sweatlodge

Ceremony. Richard had been right about her perspective—she had experiences that were certainly unique for a six year old.

I told her I thought it was cool that she got to do so many interesting things, and asked her if her friends at school thought it was cool too.

She replied, "Yeah, but sometimes they tell me that Indians are extinct." I was trying to find a response, when she sadly said, "Some kids tell me I can't be Indian, I have to be Mexican. But my friend who is Mexican says that I am an Indian, and Mexicans are better than Indians."

Talking with Abby took me back to a time I had outgrown 16 years ago. I had forgotten about the dynamic climate of recess; elementary kids could be a lot of fun, but they could also be very cruel. Sometimes they didn't know any better while other times the behavior was intentional. Either way, it was painful to remember and painful to hear from Abby. The worst part was when she told me about the time some kids came up to her and teasingly said they'd heard that Indians cut people's heads off. It was clear the incident had hurt her feelings—that she didn't understand why people would say things like that.

I didn't know how to respond. I wanted to say it wasn't her fault people were ignorant, but that's not something you tell a six-year-old. Before I had a chance to answer, Abby started telling me a different story that took our conversation in a new direction. A few minutes later, her mom came back and joined us.

My conversation with Abby made me realize I had never heard the full story of how she had come into Richard and Rachel's life, so I asked Rachel a few questions. She was also

Native American; however, she'd been born into an Apache tribe in Arizona. It wasn't until she had gone to college and joined a student organization for Indians that she learned about the Lakota traditions. She'd felt a strong connection to many of the Lakota ways and spent more time with the tribe, eventually meeting an older Lakota woman who became like a second mother to Rachel.

She explained that the Lakota have Seven Sacred Rites, one of which was the adoption of others into the tribe. The older woman had expressed interest in adopting Rachel into the Lakota family, and, after serious reflection and prayer Rachel had decided it was the right choice.

That had been over 20 years earlier, and Rachel had continued to be an important member of the Lakota family, a community of people that took great care of each other. That was why, when Abby (the biological granddaughter of Rachel's adoptive mother) had been born to a mother who was unable to raise a child, Richard and Rachel had considered adoption. They'd known it would be a major change—Rachel had already raised two boys, and both Richard and Rachel were now old enough to be Abby's grandparents—but they knew it was the right thing to do. And the decision has brought them great joy.

It is a beautiful story—from Rachel's journey into the Lakota tribe to the actual adoption—one that captured a culture rich in community, love, and tradition. It is also the kind of story that goes untold in typical, surface level, conversation where it is easier to ask simple questions than to dig deeper.

* * *

I asked Rachel how she had reacted to the things students said to Abby; she said it had been heartbreaking the first time it happened. She pointed out that she knew Abby wasn't innocent, and was just as guilty of being bratty at times, but the fact she was being treated differently for being Native American had been difficult. She explained that she and Richard had tried to counteract the incidents with education. They wanted Abby to know as much about her heritage as possible, so that she could be proud of where she came from and teach others about her culture.

This theory made sense—education is a good remedy for ignorance.

If people took the time to ask questions and get to know each other, there would be less ignorance and discrimination. Instead, we make assumptions about who they are, what they believe, and what they are capable of doing—from religion and politics, to race and everything in between.

These assumptions cause two problems—they create unnecessary pain and prevent us from connecting with interesting people. I have known Rachel for many years, but it wasn't until I sat down for a 15-minute conversation that I truly got to know her. Now I have a whole new appreciation for her and Abby.

That's what Cup 22 taught me: each person has a unique story, but you have to be willing to go beneath the surface level to find it. The real story is often very different from the story portrayed on the surface. It's as true for friends you just met (like Abby) as it is for those you've known for a long time (like

Rachel). Our meeting had me thinking I should take more time to get to know those around me a little better, to walk a metaphorical mile in their shoes.

I say metaphorical, because I could never squeeze my feet into Abby's little shoes. But there was a lot I could learn from her. The kind of lessons best learned in first grade.

Before the conversation ended, Rachel asked, with perfect mom pitch, "Abby, what does your teacher tell you to do when people are mean?" Abby's answer was simple, "Let your light shine."

We can't control the way others treat us, but that doesn't mean we let them stop us from shining. What a great lesson to learn from a six-year-old.

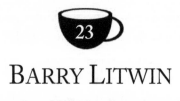

BARRY LITWIN

Wild Boar Coffee in Fort Collins, Colorado
Small house coffee

Life ain't always beautiful, but it's a beautiful ride.

I met Barry at a coffee shop in Fort Collins, Colorado—a city just 40 miles from my grandma's house, where I was staying for a few days during Christmas break before flying back to Michigan.

I'd found Barry through my high school friend Emily. A few weeks earlier, she had emailed me with information about a friend of hers I had to meet: a former Wall Street man who had worked as a trapeze artist, and was now in vet school at Colorado State University. It was a recommendation I couldn't pass up, so I sent him an email, and we set up a meeting.

I let Barry pick the location. He chose Wild Boar Coffee—the epitome of a college-town coffee shop: friendly and relaxed baristas, with a slightly offbeat feel, crowded with students behind laptops or notebooks at every table.

It was clear Barry was a regular; he'd saved a great table next to the fireplace. We sat down, and he got the conversation rolling.

"Okay, what did Emily tell you about me. We'll start with that, and then I'll fill in the gaps."

Sounded like a good idea to me. I told him the few facts I knew, and he chuckled, "All right, you're close."

He paused, collected his thoughts, and started unraveling a story that began with him as a young boy in Pennsylvania. He was one of six kids, the son of a steelworker and a mother whose aspirations of college and career had been cut short when the war had forced her to leave high school for a full-time job. Although Barry's parents hadn't had much money, they had exposed their kids to the arts and emphasized the importance of hard work and a good education.

It was mandatory that all six kids would go to college, so Barry had worked two jobs—in the botany department of the Carnegie Museum during the day and a steel mill at night—to save money to go to Penn State, where he had met a girl he followed out to California after graduation.

He had intended on marrying this girl, but—as it so often happens—life didn't go according to plan. Their relationship fell apart, and Barry had moved to Anchorage to be a flight attendant manager for a regional airline. He'd stayed for a few years before moving to the Caribbean where he worked as a dishwasher when he wasn't busy swimming in the ocean or cycling along the beach.

His parents had been appalled that their college-educated son was washing dishes, but Barry needed time to think about what he wanted in life.

He finally decided on law school—but stumbled onto a different opportunity before he got around to applying. On his way home from the Caribbean, Barry had stopped briefly to visit a close friend, a doctor in St. Louis. Barry hadn't thought much of the meeting, but a few weeks later the doctor had called to say one of his patients, a very successful stockbroker, was looking to hire an assistant.

The broker was a brilliant older man who had gone blind from an illness. When Barry sat down to hear more about the available job position, he told the broker that, in exchange for the right salary, he would be willing to commit five years to the brokerage world before continuing with his plan of attending law school.

The broker just laughed, which had caught Barry off-guard. It wasn't a typical response after accepting a job offer. But, as Barry was about to learn, this man was anything but typical; he was a difficult and high-maintenance employer. One of his co-workers would later tell Barry no prior employee had ever lasted more than one year.

It didn't take Barry long to find out why. Barry told me that if I watched Scent of a Woman, followed by The Devil Wears Prada, I would have a good sense of what it was like working for this man. Despite the pressures of the job, though, Barry endured. He had committed to five years and he wasn't about to leave early.

He had also changed his mind about law school; he decided he wanted to be a stockbroker instead. After exhausting 12-hour days, he would spend his nights studying to earn a brokerage license. When his five years were up, he left his job, joined a competitive brokerage firm in St. Louis and built a strong clientele.

He continued on, saying that while he had been working as an investment broker, he became involved with a small regional high-end circus, through charitable and cultural volunteer work. One night, he asked if he could view the tent from the trapeze-platform after a show. Once up there, the performers, whom he'd gotten to know as friends, told him (as a joke) that they wouldn't let Barry back down, unless he flew. "Okay," he said.

They harnessed him in, gave him a few tips, and let him fly. When he landed in the net at the bottom, the circus crew was in disbelief—he had perfect form, which Barry explained had come from his seven years of dance experience. The performers went on to convince him to start training as a performer. Barry was suddenly a successful stockbroker by day, and a trapeze artist by night. To top it all off, he met and married the love of his life.

Unfortunately, there was trouble on the horizon. His spouse of 12 years developed brain cancer, a battle that would be lost. We didn't talk much about their relationship or the cancer, but what Barry did have to say was poignant: having the love of his life die in his arms had changed the way he saw the world. He now appreciated life in a different way and savored each moment.

That was why, when he realized he was no longer happy after post-9/11 regulations changed the brokerage industry, he decided to change directions yet again.

A few years earlier, he'd taken a trip to visit a friend's ranch outside of St. Louis, where he discovered he had a skill for working with horses, and he had always been impressed with how the trick-riders in the circus were totally dedicated to their horses. He had developed a strong connection when he began to work with horses himself. When he was ready to leave his job, he decided to follow his passion and find a way to work with horses full time.

To Barry, it didn't matter that he would have to go back and take undergraduate classes with students half his age. It didn't matter that getting into vet school would be a major challenge, or that he would be in his mid-50s before even starting his practice. He knew with complete certainty it was the right choice, and he had the focus to make it happen.

* * *

After nearly an hour of conversation, I had finally found out how Barry had ended up in Fort Collins. His story was unlike any I had ever heard. Not only was it fascinating, he told it in a way that made me feel that anything was possible.

He relayed a piece of advice he firmly believes: "Everything happens for a reason although sometimes we don't understand the reason until much later."

Barry doesn't believe in coincidence. It might seem like his life has been a series of disjointed events and strange twists of fate, but he said that all his unique experiences had been leading him to this point in his life. And his future will be the result of hard work, ingenuity, and the courage to be open to new people and experiences.

I left the meeting with an odd feeling of tranquility. Coffee with Barry was a reminder that my life isn't going to be perfect; I will go through difficult times of uncertainty, experience painful loss, and encounter unexpected change. However, with persistence and the right attitude, life will go on, and get better.

Or as the Gary Allan country song says, *"Life ain't always beautiful, but it's a beautiful ride."*

ANGELA SHETLER

Skype call from Michigan to Japan
Venti black coffee from Starbucks

***

Get comfortable with being uncomfortable.

I'd set my alarm early enough to run to the corner Starbucks and back before nine. I hadn't gotten used to the early-morning routine of the semester, and knew waking up would require something stronger than what my puny coffeemaker could brew. Once back in my room, I sat down at my computer and got ready to chat.

Angela Shetler was also drinking coffee at her computer, and likely just as tired, but for the opposite reason. Halfway around the world, it was 11 p.m., and Angela had finished a busy day teaching English in a Japanese high school.

* * *

After graduating from Michigan State's Professional Writing Program in 2005, Angela had found a job writing copy for the American Cancer Society. She'd enjoyed her job, and she was good at it, but her husband (also an MSU grad) had wanted an adventure abroad. They knew if they waited too long to travel abroad, they'd get comfortable in their careers and never leave the U.S., So they had decided to apply to the Japan Exchange and Teaching (JET) Programme.

With the applications submitted, Angela and her husband began a waiting game, to see what the next chapter of their lives would bring. Weeks later, when the acceptance letters had arrived, they'd sold their furniture, packed their suitcases, and moved 6,000 miles away to start new jobs in a very foreign place.

Luckily, with the magic of technology, Angela had stayed connected with her American friends, which was how we had originally met. We'd found each other on Twitter and had a few friendly exchanges. Nothing substantial, but enough to know she was living in Japan. Her experience fascinated me because, although I'm fairly adventurous when it comes to traveling and moving far from home, I'm not sure I could brave moving to Japan.

I had hoped to meet up with her while she was home for the holidays, but I'd been home in Wyoming by the time she made it back to Michigan. I dreamily considered a weekend trip to Japan for coffee—but decided Skype was a much more economical option.

So that's how Angela and I shared Cup 24, which was easily one of the most peculiar Cups I'd had at that point—not because of Angela (she's great) but rather the process. After 23 Cups, I'd grown accustomed to the process of physically meeting someone new for coffee, but this meeting broke all the rules. There wasn't the typical, "Hi, are you Angela?" exchange, followed by a handshake and hello. There also wasn't a coffee-shop ambiance or the ability to read full-body body language (which was far more important than I had realized). Our conversation was confined to a pixelated image on a computer screen.

Despite the strangeness, the conversation started rolling when Angela told me about the differences between the two cultures. It was a reminder that we could get so caught up in our cultural norms that we forget people in other cultures often live vastly different lifestyles.

For example, she made the coffee she was drinking with a single-serving coffee filter placed on top of her cup as she filled it with hot water. She held it up to her camera, so I knew what she was talking about; it was a smart little contraption, and something I'd never seen in the U.S.

She explained that the Japanese don't use coffee as essential morning fuel, the way Americans do. They drank it midafternoon, and if they bought it in a store, they drank it in the store—no grabbing a cup in the middle of the afternoon commute.

They also weren't big on peanut butter, cereal, or really sweet foods (although Angela had found 43 different flavors of Kit Kats). Another surprising fact, which I found shocking, seeing as I'm a normal college kid, was that Facebook isn't big there. Japanese teens used other social networking sites that allowed for more anonymity.

Hearing about these differences was interesting, because it revealed how drastically Angela's life changed when she moved. It hadn't been just a few small changes, like coffee and technology; she had fully submerged herself in a new culture, which you can't do without getting a few bumps and bruises in the process.

When she'd left the U.S, she didn't know how to speak Japanese, which essentially made her illiterate as she tried to navigate the streets of her new home. In addition to that, blond, blue-eyed women were a rare sight in Japan. It was common to have locals stare and babies look at her in wonderment. Of course, she already had an idea of what she was getting into. Before leaving, she had done her research, and read about the four stages of culture shock, but that hadn't made it any easier. It helped that she had her husband with her. Together they had signed up for an adventure and accepted that the adjustment period was a price they'd have to pay for the experience.

Now, almost three years later, their adventure was ending, and they were preparing for a new one. Once the school year was over, they would be moving to Australia, where Angela would pursue a Master's degree. Her original plan for grad school had been going back to MSU. She was comfortable with the school and knew it was a good option. But that was before the Japan experience.

When I asked her how moving to Japan had changed her, she said this, "The experience has made me comfortable with being uncomfortable."

Three years ago, she hadn't had what it would take to move to Australia for grad school. But challenging herself to move to Japan revealed her strengths and capabilities. Overcoming the struggles helped her realize she could tackle more than she thought.

I could relate to her statement. I had left the Wyoming town I grew up in for the unknowns of Michigan, and I faced a few hurdles of my own in the transition. Despite that, I ultimately had an incredible experience in Michigan, and learned that so often the most rewarding things in life were those that were the most challenging.

* * *

While I had previously learned the value of trying new things firsthand, I enjoyed the reminder. The thing about change is that if you wait long enough, the uncomfortable eventually becomes comfortable. After four years, I felt right at home in Michigan and the idea of uprooting to a new location and starting from scratch again frankly wasn't appealing.

I had discovered this resistance to moving a few days before meeting with Angela, and it scared me a little. I had been planning on moving to a big city, so when the idea of staying closer to the familiar Midwest popped into my head, I was surprised and a little worried. *Was I losing my courage? Was I thinking about settling? Was I actually considering the comfortable route over the adventurous one?*

Cup 24 is a reminder that you have to work constantly to stay comfortable with being uncomfortable. This doesn't necessarily mean moving to a foreign country, like Angela did. It means staying open to trying new things, taking risks, and finding new challenges instead of getting stuck in the comfortable routines of life. The ability to explore difficult situations is like a muscle; if you stop exercising it, the strength goes away.

If I start choosing the easy route over the one with a few twists and turns, I might never discover just how far I can go.

BETSY MINER-SWARTZ

Edmund's Pastime in Lansing, Michigan
Small house coffee

When life gets tough, take it one step at a time.

By the time I got to the Edmund's, I was 15 minutes late and flustered from an unexpectedly hectic afternoon. I called to let Betsy know of my delay, but that didn't loosen the knot in my stomach, knowing I'd potentially ruined a first impression.

I rushed into the restaurant and spotted Betsy immediately. She was patiently waiting at a booth, basking in the warm sunlight streaming in from the tall windows facing Michigan Avenue, cup of coffee in hand.

"Betsy! I am so sorry for being late!"

Her response was untroubled and lifted the worry off my shoulders, "I think there are worse things than having to sit and enjoy a cup of coffee for 15 minutes." I knew immediately I was going to like Betsy, and with the mayhem of the day behind me, I was ready to slow down and enjoy good coffee in good company.

* * *

Betsy is a communications specialist with Gift of Life Michigan. Since 2009, she has worked diligently to promote statewide organ-, eye- and tissue-donation and grow the

Michigan Organ Donor Registry. It is an important job, because Michigan has fallen behind the national average in terms of number of registered donors. Michigan also has 2,993 residents waiting for transplants.

As we were discussing the nature of the issue, Betsy fidgeted with her cell phone, which had a "Donate Life" sticker prominently displayed on the back; tt was clear the organization meant more than just a job to her.

* * *

In 1986, Betsy graduated with a Journalism degree from Central Michigan University. Three days later, she found herself navigating the real-world newsroom at the Sturgis Journal. She'd known she wanted to be a journalist since high school, and had been determined to build a strong career. It wasn't long before her writing skills and work ethic landed her a gig in Port Huron, then later at the Lansing State Journal.

For more than 15 years, she worked at the State Journal, moving up through the news ranks, collecting awards and accolades along the way. After a series of promotions, Betsy found herself running the news desk—feeling more pressure than ever before.

It had been the most challenging role of her career, especially with the uncertain future of print media, but Betsy had always been able to handle high-stress situations. She knew she could make it work.

But then, something happened in her personal life that changed everything. In 2005, her father was diagnosed with pancreatic cancer.

The diagnosis had been completely unexpected. At age 67, Betsy's father had been in great health. He should have had years of life left to live. It was difficult news to receive, and Betsy, the oldest of three daughters, responded by taking an active role in his treatment and providing support for her mother.

It soon became clear she had too much on her plate. That's when Betsy's partner of seven years, Robin Miner-Swartz, encouraged Betsy to do something she would never have considered: quit her job. Robin also worked at the State Journal, a job that offered full benefits for domestic partners. It was a big decision, and one Betsy was grateful Robin helped her make. She turned in her resignation letter and shifted her priorities to what mattered.

As Betsy said, if you have to get cancer, pancreatic isn't the type you want to choose. She braced herself for the worst and, sadly, lost her father in 2006. Then, as if dealing with the loss of her father hadn't been hard enough, her 66-year-old mother was diagnosed with Stage IV ovarian cancer a year and a half later. She passed away in 2009.

It was impossible for me to fathom what it must have been like going through such an experience. I wasn't sure how to respond, but I eventually settled on asking her how she'd done it—how she'd climbed the Mount Everest of life challenges.

Her answer was simple: "I focused on one thing at a time."

She said she would choose one thing—the most-important thing on her to-do list—and then do it. That might have been taking a shower or driving to the funeral home to plan a funeral. When she finished that task, she moved on to the next important one. She wouldn't think about the bigger picture because it was too overwhelming; the stress would have broken her down.

Today, as she looks back, it is clear the experience has changed her outlook on life. Her priorities have changed. As Betsy said, "Grief shapes us." Without the adversity in her career and personal life, she wouldn't have been able to appreciate the satisfying life she now has. Each day, she wakes up thankful for another day and the blessings it brings.

Betsy also said she firmly believes that everything happens for a reason. While losing her parents was the hardest thing she has ever endured, without that experience, she wouldn't have quit her job, and if she hadn't quit her job, she would never have found the opportunity with Gift of Life Michigan, a role that allows her to help save lives every day.

* * *

Grief, heartache, and loss are inevitable; we can't predict what will happen or when. However, what I learned from Betsy is that we get to choose how we are going to deal with the challenges that life brings. Betsy proves it is possible to tackle adversity head-on, and find strength to keep going until the worst is over. Cup 25 provides inspiration to keep going despite the circumstances.

I know that life will throw twists and turns my way—that I'll encounter plenty of rough spots along my journey—but keeping Betsy's story with me will be a powerful reminder that, with the right attitude and the right people at my side, I can find the strength to endure anything. It's just a matter of focusing on one thing at a time.

JIM LITTLE

H&H Mobil in East Lansing, Michigan
Medium brewed coffee, hazelnut blend

It's nice to have a place where everybody knows your name.

The epic "Snowpocalypse" snowstorm of 2011 descended upon East Lansing, closing down schools and interrupting my original plans to head to Detroit for Cup 26 in the process.

Unsure of how to carry out the week's coffee plan, I looked at the 11 inches of snow, through which I would have to trudge and remembered hearing a story about how Jim Little, the owner of H&H Mobil, had once voluntarily plowed my friend's driveway after a last major snowfall. Included in my friend's story was helpful advice: "You're a business major—if you want to know about customer service, he's the guy to talk to!"

So I decided to call up H&H and ask for Jim. I apologized for the late notice and asked if he'd be willing to meet for coffee the next day. He said he's at the shop from 7 a.m. to 7 p.m. daily, so he'd be around if I stopped by. I said I'd see him at 10:30

While coffee shops have the ambiance and magnetic power of caffeine that draws me in on a daily basis, gas stations are places I only frequent when my gas warning light yells at me. I find them dingy, unwelcoming, and overly fluorescent. When

I do get a fill-up, I typically pay at the pump and quickly go on my way.

Nevertheless, the idea of sharing a cup of coffee outside my usual realm is was intriguing. As I drove to the store, I hoped my intuition didn't let me down.

I walked into the station to find Jim talking with two customers. He said hello and I introduced myself before he pointed me toward the coffee and told me to help myself. With a coffee in hand, we found a spot in an unoccupied corner of the store—between the bathroom and the pop machine—where he asked me outright, "Well, what do you want to know?"

* * *

Jim, like me, had studied business at Michigan State. After graduation, he had set his sights on going back into the Navy as a pilot, but the uncertainty of the Vietnam War had prompted him to put his business degree to work instead. He'd heard about the opportunity to buy a new Mobil Oil station on the corner of Hagadorn and Haslett roads, and decided to venture into entrepreneurship. He had previous experience working in gas stations and figured it would be a good undertaking for a couple of years. He bought the shop, and named it Hagadorn and Haslett Mobil (quickly shortened to H&H); 41 years later, he was still running the business.

Jim is in his late 60s and works in the store about 12 hours a day, five days a week, plus a handful of hours on the weekend. He told me his wife can't figure out where he gets all his energy.

For my part, I can't figure out how anyone could look so happy with a work schedule like his. However, the longer I am in the store, the more it made sense. When I asked him if, after 40 years in business, his customers felt like family, he gave a knowing chuckle and motioned me to follow him to where two customers were standing by the candy bars, shooting the breeze while their cars were being serviced. He interrupted them, "Guys, would you say I know most of my customers?" The hearty response from the man, later introduced as Chuck, said it all: "Oh yeah! This is a neighborhood store; everyone I know comes here." The other man, amusingly also named Chuck, agreed. They'd clearly been loyal customers for years.

Jim and I walked back to the corner to continue our conversation, which was interrupted moments later as the general conversation in the shop shifted to the impending boat season. Jim wanted to contribute his two cents, and then the talk somehow moved to flying. Jim mentioned he liked to fly his plane to various vacation spots; the woman behind the counter chimed in that while it was a fun plane to fly, landing it was another story.

I soon realized the woman behind the counter was Jim's wife. They had met long ago when she started working at the station. And that's when I figured out Jim worked so much while staying happy: H&H was more than just his job and his business; it was his social life, his family, and where he felt most at home. After just 20 minutes, the camaraderie in the shop had won me over.

I was quietly observing the proceedings—taking note of how it oddly felt like I was as in the middle of a sitcom—when suddenly an employee behind the counter answered a call. There was a car stuck on the train tracks. With the three other towing guys out on calls, it was Jim's job to go get it moved. With the agility of a man half his age, Jim sprung into action. He rushed out of the shop to check on something, and then ran back in, calling through the open door, "You want to come? You can see how I spend my days!"

I sprinted out of the store caught completely off-guard by the drastic change of events. I tossed my coffee into one of the bins by the pump, as I watched Jim quickly look both ways before rushing across the busy street. He then held back traffic so I could follow him across to the impound lot.

We jumped into his truck and were on our way out of the lot, when an update came through the radio. The car—luckily—was no longer stuck.

We parked the truck and walked back to the station. My heartbeat slowly returned to normal, along with the conversation. I asked Jim what he had learned after 40 years in business. He replied, "Work hard, stay healthy, and have good luck." It was basic advice, but it was advice that had been good to Jim.

His business model was just as simple. His secret to success was to be there when people dropped their cars off in the morning and to be there when they picked them up at night. He always said thank you, treated his customers right, and did his best to offer a quality product. He didn't advertise; he didn't need to.

Our conversation ended when an older man, probably somewhere in his 80s, walked in and said hello. He'd brought his car in for service. Jim told him to grab a coffee; he'd give him a ride home in a second. Cleary this wasn't the first time Jim had given him a ride, and I was sure he'd go back to pick him up once his car was finished.

* * *

As I walked back to my car, I reflected on the experience with satisfaction that it had, in fact, been as chaotic and interesting as I'd hoped. However, it wasn't until later that day when the disjointed events at H&H made sense.

I decided to take my neglected, winter-worn car for a much-needed oil change. I could have had H&H do it, but old habits die hard and, without a second thought, I headed down the road to the franchise service shop I'd visited at least a dozen times. Despite my many trips, when I walked inside, the service man asked if I had ever been there before.

It happened every time. And never has anyone there remembered my name, offered me a ride, or asked about my family. They knew me as a 1998 Jeep Grand Cherokee, not as Megan, the loyal customer. I instantly regretted not going back to H&H.

* * *

As the characters in *Cheers* know, it's nice to have a place where everybody (or at least somebody) knows your name— especially in today's increasingly technological world with self-checkout, pay-at-the-pump, online banking, online shopping, email, and more. Life is faster than ever, but it can also be isolating.

Jim's story shows the power of going out of your way to make a connection with someone—to say hello, to listen, to offer a cup of coffee.

I know I'll be back to H&H. Because when life is going a hundred miles an hour and getting gas is the last thing I want to do, it would be nice to hear someone say, "Thanks for stopping in, Megan, and have a great day."

27

Masaki Takahashi

Wanderer's Teahouse in East Lansing, Michigan
Small green tea

Forgiveness is hard, but better than a lifetime of resentment.

Cup 27 started with an unexpected email. The student-run newspaper at Michigan State had printed a story about my 52 Cups project, and Masaki Takahashi, who just happened to stumble across it, felt compelled to email me.

The last line of his email hooked me: "I love the idea of the blog because I am on my own mission to branch out as well. I have kept this guard up from letting people into my life and am hoping to let it down."

The message resonated with me—big time. One of the greatest things that had happened to me during college has been learning to let my walls down. I came into college as a reserved freshman, but because I was a thousand miles from home, I had to eventually open up to the people around me. Luckily, I made incredible supportive friends and learned that the more I open up, the better life gets.

I decided I had to meet him.

* * *

When I walked into the teashop, I found him waiting at the counter. I introduced myself, and we ordered tea (which, although a deviation from my coffee-norm, I allowed due to our location), and found a place to sit down. The teashop was crowded but had a comfortable atmosphere conducive to good conversation. After a few minutes of small talk, I asked him to tell me a little bit about himself.

It took him three sentences to answer my question, "Well, I'm a Media Arts major. I'm a junior. I have a four-year-old son; that's about it."

Two things about his response caught me off-guard. First of all, I would never have guessed this young 20-something student would have a son. And secondly, he was so nonchalant with his answer: Three sentences and a "that's about it"? I knew there had to be more.

In his defense, he had told me he was good at keeping his walls up. Luckily, as I continued to ask him questions, he opened up and his incredible story eventually came out.

* * *

Masaki's high-school sweetheart had gotten pregnant during their freshman year of college. It was an unexpected event and a scary time for both of them, but they married, and Masaki shifted his focus to doing everything necessary to take care of his new family. They needed money, so he started working 80 hours a week, eventually dropping out of school because he couldn't juggle a family, job, and classes.

While the constant work kept food on the table, it took a toll on his new marriage. He thought he was doing the right thing—providing financial support—but keeping the family together took more than just money. The strain of the situation eventually became too much, and Masaki and his wife decided to split up.

As he told me this, it was evident he was disappointed—both because he had lost someone he truly loved, and because he felt like he'd let his family and himself down. In the process of this story, he explained, "I think I failed because I had never seen it done right."

It wasn't an excuse, nor was he passing the blame to someone else. He was simply stating a fact: he had grown up in a rocky household and didn't know what a stable family looked like; let alone how to create one.

* * *

Masaki was born in Japan and had never known his father. At the age of four, his mother, overwhelmed with single-motherhood, had sent him to live with his aunt and uncle in America.

The transition from life in Japan to life in America—without his mom by his side—had been inevitably difficult. And while the situation was better than life in Japan, it wasn't ideal. His uncle struggled with alcohol, and his new home lacked praise and encouragement.

By age 16, Masaki had developed some behavioral problems (in his words, he was a 'brat'), and his aunt and uncle weren't equipped to deal with these problems. They kicked him out of the house, sending him back to Japan to live with his mom.

So once again, he was shuffled across the world to a new environment. After being away for ten years—not to mention that adolescence was already a difficult period in one's life—reconnecting with his mom was an interesting experience. Overall, he enjoyed the experience and the freedom he had to explore the city, before eventually returning to his aunt and uncle's home in the U.S., graduating from high school and then enrolling at Michigan State.

Had I known his history in advance, I probably would have been expecting to meet a resentful, overwhelmed man. Let alone a man juggling split-custody of a four-year-old ("the coolest kid in the world"), a full course load and two jobs. That's a lot for one man to handle.

But Masaki's disposition showed no trace of a stressful life. He is enthusiastic, gracious, and has a great outlook on life. I asked him how he did it—how he kept going when life got so hard. How he stayed on the right path when, without anyone supporting him, he could have so easily gone down a much darker path?

His answers gave true insight into his character. He said he felt like he had something to prove to the world—and I could see the drive in his eyes. One day, he said he wanted to look back at the years of struggling and see that all his pain had been worth it. He was driven by the idea that a better life awaited him and his son, and if he could endure long enough, he would find it.

But, in the meantime, he persists and holds onto his optimism. As he said, "As long as there's a tomorrow, life is all right."

* * *

As I talked with Masaki, I kept thinking about a quote I'd heard once: *Life is not holding a good hand; Life is playing a poor hand well.*

If I'd learned anything in my first six months of coffees, it's that nobody is dealt a perfect hand; we all have a unique set of challenges. Seeing Masaki's unwavering drive for a better life, despite his struggles, was an inspiration.

Masaki has many people in his past he could understandably be angry with, but a major lesson he'd learned is that harboring pain and anger only makes you bitter. Instead of holding onto the resentment of his childhood, he was looking for the strength to forgive and move on.

Resentment is something that builds up easily—whether from a major incident or small ones gradually accumulating over time. As it builds, it starts to weigh us down, hindering us from moving forward.

It can happen unconsciously, which is why I appreciated my conversation with Masaki. It prompted me to think about my own burdens, the hatchets I had been meaning to bury.

Masaki invited me to coffee as a way to let his walls down, and in the process, he showed me that there were some I was still holding up.

28

ELLEN KAY

Bean and Leaf Café in Royal Oak, Michigan
Medium green tea

People may not say thank you, but that doesn't mean your efforts aren't appreciated.

Ellen Kay has a challenging job. She teaches first grade at an elementary school in Macomb County, a suburb of Detroit.

I can't imagine trying to capture the attention of a couple dozen six- and seven-year-olds, and then keeping it long enough to cover the principles of basic math and proper nouns. I'm just not fit for the elementary-school scene, which was why I admire those who have a passion for it.

And that was before I had even met Ellen. Hearing her story increased my admiration, while simultaneously creating an urge to send thank-you letters to the elementary teachers in my life who have truly made a difference.

Ellen works at a school where many of the children are living at or below the poverty line. Her greatest challenge is getting the students to practice their reading at home—and over the summer—but for many of their parents, there are higher priorities than taking 15 minutes to sit and read a book, especially for the few students who don't have permanent homes.

That is just one difficulty. She also has to deal with standardized testing, ever increasing class sizes, and decreasing attention spans—all interfering with her passion for educating students and preparing them for their futures.

* * *

Ellen Kay was telling me about her experience as a teacher while we sat in an adorable cafe, filled with a varied clientele of students studying, people meeting to talk business, and others just enjoying coffee on a sunny afternoon. Ellen was a little reserved, but amiable and engaging. It was a pleasant conversation. I had a hard time wrapping my head around the difficult job of teaching students who were facing such difficult situations.

She acknowledged that her job wasn't easy, and there are a lot of tough days, but the kids kept her going. She knew she could make a difference in their lives—because she had teachers that had made a difference in hers.

Ellen planned to become an architect, but it was a third-grade teacher who changed her mind. While in high school, an elementary school teacher needed a volunteer to spend an hour in her classroom once a week, and it was Ellen who filled the role. Through the experience she discovered a love for teaching and changed her plans for college.

It is a decision she is still happy about. For some of her students, she had been their only source of support and encouragement. Seeing her students learn and grow made it easier for her to overlook the imperfections of the school system.

At least for now, anyway. Ellen Kay has seen how the stress of the job wears people down and makes them bitter. She said if she ever reached that point, she would leave teaching. There are students who depend on her; she knows she has the power to change lives, but she only wants to change them if it is a change for the better.

I respect her for that; although I've had incredible teachers in my academic career, I've also had some who clearly no longer found joy in their jobs. As Ellen spoke, I couldn't help but think back to my memories of elementary school—from the first day of school with my backpack stocked with a fresh set of Crayola crayons, to the weekly trips to the library, the made-up recess games, and the awful food they fed us at lunch. Those were the days when homework assignments consisted of craft projects, and every holiday was a cause for celebration and cupcakes.

Looking back, I realize the excitement of school was just a bunch of new knowledge, cleverly disguised as fun. I couldn't appreciate what my teachers did for me until much later, after I'd moved on to the next step of my life. As a society, we too often underappreciate teachers, even though they can be some of the most important people in our lives.

But that lack of appreciation doesn't stop teachers from working hard, which is the lesson I will take away from Cup 28. Sometimes, a work situation isn't ideal. Sometimes, it takes a lot of work before you see a payoff. And sometimes, your efforts may go unnoticed.

But if it is for a worthy cause—if it is something that changes the world, even invisibly—it is worth doing. And it is worth doing right.

29

SUE CARTER

Biggby Coffee in East Lansing, Michigan
Small house coffee

"The water buffalo are waiting at the gate. Let's go!"

This was a common phrase Sue Carter heard while growing up. It was one of her mother's favorites: an expression that implied there was a whole world outside waiting to be discovered and she wasn't going to find it sitting inside.

The mentality had clearly passed on to Sue. In 2001, she led the first all-women expedition to the North Pole. Then she wrote a book about it.

In March of 2010, she traveled to Malawi, Africa, to document the efforts of Michigan State University Professor Terrie Taylor and her team's decade-long effort to study and understand the nature of childhood malaria.

As a journalism professor at Michigan State for the past two decades, she spent each summer taking a group of young minds to the United Kingdom for a once-in-a-lifetime study-abroad experience.

All of these experiences were on top of a 17-year career as a broadcast journalist, during which she earned various accolades, including UPI Sports Broadcaster of the Year and an Emmy for her documentary, *The Great Experiment*. In April of 2007, she was inducted into the Michigan Journalism Hall of

Fame. And, as if that weren't enough, she had also obtained a law degree from Wayne State University, and later became an ordained priest.

But if you met Sue in person, you would never suspect this warm-hearted woman in her sixties would have such a remarkable number of experiences under her belt. I only knew because a mutual friend insisted we talk. He described her as the "textbook definition of living your dreams joyfully and totally." As soon as he told me this, I emailed to see if she'd be able to meet.

A week later, I was sitting across from Sue in a crowded coffee shop listening to her various stories and the lessons she learned in the process.

I wondered about her trek to the North Pole, so I asked her to tell me what had spurred the grand idea. Turns out, it all happened over a simple cup of coffee. She was meeting with a friend who mentioned recently joining a team of women going to the North Pole. That was an adventure right up Sue's alley; "Not without me, you're not!" she responded. Then she found a way to join the crew.

She explained that, when it comes to life, you have to be present, sign up, and make opportunities happen instead of waiting for them to arrive. Like Woody Allen said: *Eighty percent of life is just showing up.*

However, the North Pole trip wasn't meant to be. The team encountered roadblock after roadblock, and the plans were canceled. That didn't stop Sue. Something about the trip had struck a chord within and she knew she needed to continue pursuing the goal. After a short break, she took charge, and, after nearly eight years of planning, the trip became a reality. Twelve women skied from Russia to the North Pole, enduring incredible physical, environmental, and personal challenges during the 130-mile expedition.

The trip was a lesson in perseverance and trusting intuition. Success might not appear exactly as expected or within the desired time frame, but with persistence, faith, and hard work, things eventually come together.

And sometimes they come together in interesting ways. When they had reached the North Pole, a team from NASA had been waiting to do an international webcast before taking them home. Sue had a longtime friend who worked for NASA. She had been meaning to go visit the friend for years, but hadn't found the time. Serendipitously, that friend had been put on the helicopter team, and the two friends had the chance to reconnect—at the North Pole of all places!

That was one of the many serendipitous moments in Sue's life. A few years earlier, she realized that she was being called to the ministry and had taken a sabbatical from teaching to move to New York to become ordained within the Episcopal Church. She befriended a man from Africa in one of her classes, but they lost touch after she moved back to Michigan. However, when Sue traveled to Malawi, to film a documentary on Professor Taylor's work with malaria, she discovered she was in the same city as her friend, and she was able to reconnect with him halfway around the world from where they'd originally met.

* * *

I loved hearing Sue recount these small-world experiences. I'm constantly amazed at those situations where everything seems to fall into place like magic, as if the stars had aligned perfectly to make a certain situation happen. It is an exhilarating feeling and one that has happened to me a few times over the previous six months of 52 Cups.

Sue calls these experiences moments that are "rightly ordered." During these moments, the countless pieces of our lives are in sync—in proper alignment—and the result is that things fall into place. Being in a "rightly ordered" state is a good place to be.

I asked her how one creates a situation that is rightly ordered.

Sue explained that these moments may seem like coincidence, but there is more to them than just chance. Rightly ordered situations are affirmations of the choices we make. When things come together, it is a sign that we are on the right road, that we are making the right decisions.

It was reassuring to hear that if you pay attention to the surroundings, the world gives you feedback. And it works with both good and bad choices: If the signs around you don't feel right, and nothing seems to be going well, there is something out of alignment and it's a good time to reevaluate your decisions.

* * *

We continued talking, and Sue continued to pass along great pieces of advice and share great stories. It felt like I was sitting with an old friend I'd known for years. When our meeting ended and we parted ways, I felt a great sense of calm. It was partly from her warm and selfless nature and partly from her advice.

One of the many lessons I will take away from Cup 29 is that life is dynamic and always providing feedback. When you make a decision, you can read the signs and readjust if necessary. It is a great mindset because it reduces much of the fear caused by the uncertainty of what the future holds. It takes a certain level of faith, but with the right approach to life, and the courage to change course when necessary, everything works out in the end. Living in fear of what might lay in the future only holds us back. And I don't have time for that.

The water buffalo are waiting at the gate.

MIKE MCFALL

Biggby Coffee Headquarters in East Lansing, Michigan
Small house coffee

Embrace uncertainty; it keeps life interesting.

"Do you ever wonder how your life would be if you had made one decision differently?" Mike McFall asked me this question as we sat in his office at the Headquarters of Biggby Coffee, a popular Midwestern coffee chain.

The question came after he'd recounted the events that led him to spend a year of high school sailing around the world for a study-at-sea experience. His mom had picked up a brochure about the program thinking Mike might be interested. Mike was slightly intrigued, so he filled out the application and threw it on his coffee table—where it sat for weeks, forgotten amongst the various items coffee tables tend to accumulate.

While sitting on the couch one afternoon, his mother uncovered the application and consulted Mike, "Do you still want to do this, or should I toss it?"

Mike figured since he had filled it out; he might as well mail it. The decision changed his life. It was, unsurprisingly, an incredible experience that shaped his perspective, introduced him to new ideas, and ultimately helped him get into a very selective college despite his lackluster grades. He often asked himself afterward, *"How would my life be different if I had just let my mom toss the application?"*

* * *

We were sitting in Mike's office, a room with a round table and chairs with bare walls (he had recently moved in and hadn't gotten around to decorating). When I had arrived, he gave me a quick tour of the office that ended at the mock Biggby store where new franchise owners learn the ropes.

He told me the story of his experience at sea after I mentioned that one of the most-important lessons I had learned so far during 52 Cups had been that life never goes according to plan. Mike understood what I meant immediately. Living in Lansing, Michigan and working as the President of Biggby Coffee hadn't been in his forecast when he'd graduated from Kalamazoo College in 1994.

A research project had brought him to Lansing. While working 20 hours a week on the project, he had an abundance of time and scarcity of money so he dropped off an application at every coffee shop in town. He ended up at Biggby, which, at the time, was a small one-store operation that sold about 300 cups a day.

He'd been working there a couple of months when one day he went for a walk with the co-founder, Bob Fish. He didn't explain the details—and I didn't ask because I liked the mystique of the story—but the walk had turned into a four-hour ordeal that ended with an agreement between Mike and Bob to expand their small coffee business together.

Ten years later, they had grown to over 100 stores selling 33,000 cups a day.

Mike's story captivated me. I loved when people jumped on a big opportunity without knowing where it would lead. That's what I had done my whole life, and it had led to remarkable experiences.

We continued talking about the uncertainty of life, specifically regarding career paths. Mike mentioned something I understood immediately, "People follow the path—corporate job, marriage, kids, mortgage, etc.—because it's a safer route."

Uncertainty is difficult; it's easier to follow the route many have taken before.

That's something I'd discovered in the previous six months. There isn't a rulebook when you're paving your own way; you've got to make your own decisions and live with the unpredictability of where those decisions lead. That's a lot of pressure, which explains why we all too often opt for the path of least resistance.

Back when I started 52 Cups, I was planning on finding a corporate job like everyone expected I would. I was stuck in the mindset that there was just one route to success, and if I didn't find that *one specific route*, I would be setting myself up for irreversible failure. But 52 Cups has helped me realize that is not the case at all.

Life is what you make it—and *you* get to make it whatever you want.

* * *

I used to look for ways to make the fear of uncertainty go away, but failed every time. The reality is that life is unpredictable: the uncertainty never goes away.

Choosing to live an unconventional life means more risk and less certainty. It is the price you pay for the opportunity to make a remarkable life.

Mike agrees. He has spent his whole life living unconventionally; he has never been able to follow the crowd, and it is clear his strategy has paid off.

Cup 30 is a reminder that you can't predict what opportunities life will bring—like a parent making a recommendation for a life-changing experience, or an unexpected walk turning into something more—but the unpredictable moments are the ones that keep life interesting and fun.

KENYATTA BERRY

Phone call from East Lansing, Michigan to Los Angeles, California
Homemade brewed coffee

It's all right to strike out a few times.

In college, Kenyatta Berry found herself on academic probation. It wouldn't be the first time, and it wasn't because she
wasn't smart. In high school, she had gone to a Detroit mag-
net school for gifted kids and was always interested in
learning. She just had better things to worry about than
grades. Eventually, she got her grades into good enough shape
to earn a degree in Business Administration from Michigan
State (which is how we had a mutual friend who suggested we
meet). Then she headed to law school.

It was during her time in law school that she discovered
the then-emerging technological phenomenon called the
Internet. Kenyatta hadn't understood what it was, or what it
would become, but she knew she wanted to be a part of it. She
geared her law classes toward Intellectual Property and Patent
Law, and helped start a student group focused on Internet
Law.

She was active and driven, yet her grades weren't cutting
it—once again, she was placed on academic probation. Unfortunately, that wasn't her biggest worry. During her senior year,
her law school had a controversial racial issue that prompted

Kenyatta to send an audacious email to the student body, which she had also copied to the dean of the college.

He was not impressed by her bold action. He threatened a defamation suit, which led to a host of issues and problems that (fortunately) were worked out without a lawsuit. At the end of the year, Kenyatta walked to the Wailing Wall (the spot where grades were posted) to discover her grades were sufficient to graduate. She'd happily collected her degree and moved on to the next stage of her life without looking back.

Kenyatta had been set on getting a job in the tech industry, specifically one in Washington, D.C. She called the company every day, and her persistence paid off. The company offered her a job, so she picked up and moved to D.C. where she worked until the dot-com crash terminated both her job and the company. Fortunately, she wasn't unemployed long before finding an opening at a small company called Blackboard. Although she was greatly overqualified, she had taken the position and quickly rose through the ranks as Blackboard became a leader in online platforms for education.

After five years, Kenyatta realized she needed a change and decided to leave the company. When she quit Blackboard, she didn't have a plan, but she wasn't worried. She knew her experience working for Blackboard would be one that opened a lot of doors in her future. Plus she was resourceful. She soon took a job with a different Internet company in Massachusetts exploring her true passion: genealogy.

Before long, she had become fascinated with the idea of tracing her roots and decided to make it the center of her professional life—she decided to start a company of her own.

In the process of looking for funding for her company, an investor gave her some valuable advice. Kenyatta was most interested in genealogy focused on slavery. The investors in Massachusetts weren't interested in touching a sensitive issue like slavery and had told her she needed to move to California where the strong entrepreneurial environment might create more opportunities for her idea. Without hesitation, she packed up and moved across the country to put her idea in motion.

It was a smart move. Kenyatta found a job with another education company in Los Angeles to support her financially while she grew her company.

* * *

The rest of Kenyatta's story is unwritten. Where her company and the genealogy passion will take her is uncertain, but she is excited to find out. Despite the ups and downs of college, the short stints of unemployment, company changes, and multiple moves, Kenyatta has built a life that she greatly enjoys. It is filled with meaningful employment and opportunities to pursue her passion, helping others in the process. She may have gotten a few bumps and bruises along the way, but she has overcome the mistakes and close encounters with failure that have stood in her way.

That is an important takeaway for me, especially since growing up, I had perfect grades and rarely stepped out of line.

I explained to Kenyatta how our mindsets differed and asked how she had handled so many strikes against her. Her response will stick with me: "Everything is a learning experience."

Each of her academic and personal struggles taught her something that made her stronger for the next challenge or stumbling block. Her experiences had made her resilient, and she knows she will never encounter a defeat that is too large for her to recover. It is this reservoir of resilience that makes her unstoppable and able to push boundaries.

Kenyatta's story illustrates how to be comfortable with failure. This doesn't mean trying to fail, or being okay with it, but rather accepting failure as a common ingredient in life—not the end of the world.

I realized that I had stayed in line and worked hard so external sources could validate me: good grades proved that I was smart; no major failures meant I was a success. But if I continued to build that life, I might never experience failure, never have the chance to build my own reservoir of resilience.

Kenyatta taught me the value of looking inward to find validation, based on self-awareness and past experiences. If you can do that, you can create confidence and resilience that fosters risk taking, because you know that failure doesn't mean you aren't good enough, it just means you need to get up and attack the challenge again.

WANDA HERNDON

Starbucks in Seattle, Washington
Grande house coffee

Never underestimate the power of choice.

I spent every spring break in college visiting my brother, which meant a trip to Seattle was in store for my spring. Considering Seattle is the birthplace of Starbucks and their caffeine revolution, it only made sense to have coffee with someone who was a part of that magic.

I found the perfect person: the former Senior Vice President of Global Communications for Starbucks

* * *

Wanda Herndon has an impressive resume. After graduating with a journalism degree from Michigan State, she realized journalism wasn't the right route for her and decided to try her hand at Public Relations. Wanda set her sights on a successful corporate career and soon found herself advancing through various positions at Fortune 500 Companies, before ultimately ending up at Starbucks in Seattle.

After 11 years at Starbucks, Wanda left and started W Communications, a strategic communications consulting firm, where she takes on one client at a time. The setup keeps her working but leaves plenty of room for traveling and enjoying the life she worked so hard to create.

I found Wanda through a friend who met her in 2002 when she received the highly regarded Distinguished Alumni Award from Michigan State. When I looked into the award, I discovered it wasn't the first of her accolades. She had been named one of the twelve leading African Americans in public relations by *PR Week* magazine and one of the "Top 100 Black Professionals in Corporate America" by *Black Professionals* magazine. She was also a frequent public speaker among her many other honors and activities.

Wanda spent the hour we shared together passing along advice garnered from years of experience in the working world—advice I needed to hear. Rita Meyer, Cup Two, had told me early on that young women need more positive female role models—more examples of bold women setting the bar high and reaching their goals. After talking with Wanda, I saw the value in Rita's sentiment.

What I noticed very quickly was that Wanda didn't make excuses. I admired her candid, no-nonsense, approach to life.

I asked her how she dealt with the stress of being in a senior-level position. She told me she'd always been a good multitasker and had developed better skills as she advanced through positions.

I asked her how she found confidence as a young professional in intimidating business situations. She said she worked hard and paid attention to what others were doing. If she ran into a tough project, she executed it to the best of her ability and then looked for ways to do better the next time.

I asked her how she kept moving forward when life got overwhelming. Her response was just to hang in there; tomorrow would bring a new day—maintaining patience, diligence, and perseverance was the key.

Wanda told me that there would always be people telling me that I'm not good enough and that I shouldn't allow myself to add negative self-talk as it only adds fuel to their fire. She said I should be my biggest fan, cheerleader, and promoter, and I should stand up for myself and believe I could do it.

Her mentality was like a Nike commercial: *Just Do It.* And that was just the beginning. Wanda continued to share more insights, which culminated in this take-away: "Life is about choices."

*　*　*

The situation you are in right now, whatever it might be, is the direct result of the choices you made in the past. Where you are next week, next year, or next decade will be the result of the choices you make today.

Life is not the product of the environment, the economy, the weather, what your friends are doing, or what your boss wants. Life is about what *you choose* to do under those circumstances.

Considering the next six months of my life would be full of choices, Wanda's perspective was indispensable from a variety of reasons.

First, she reminded me that we all have to make decisions we don't want to make: The fear of making the wrong choice sometimes incapacitates our decision-making abilities. We procrastinate; hoping someone or something will come along and make the choice for us. Wanda isn't the type of woman who takes a passive stance when it comes to deciding which direction to take her life next; she has great confidence and is bold in her decision-making. If she makes the wrong decision, she quickly makes a correction.

Very few choices are permanent.

Her advice reminded me of my college search. I was so overwhelmed and worried about deciding on the right college. When my mom told me, "Megan, don't let the choice create so much anxiety. If you pick a college and hate it, you can transfer." Like magic, her advice lifted a weight off my shoulders.

* * *

After talking with Wanda, I realized the real mistake isn't making the wrong choice; it is failing to change course once you realize a choice was wrong. This is what Wanda meant when she said people underestimated the control they have over their lives. All too often, people get stuck in a bad spot and don't take action to get out.

Whether it is a dead-end job, an unhealthy relationship, financial trouble, poor health or something else, people fail to realize they have the power to make choices that can change the situation.

Maybe we're afraid of how people will react to our actions. We get caught up thinking our behavior needs to fall in line with others' expectations. But, as Wanda said, "Ignore the expectations others have for you. Create expectations for yourself and focus on those because if you reach your expectations, I guarantee you'll be exceeding the expectations other have for you."

* * *

When I walked away from my meeting with Wanda, I was overcome with a great feeling: a mix of energy and relief. Yes, I had a lot of decisions to make in the next six months—heck; I have a lot of decisions to make in the next 60 years! But talking to Wanda made those decisions seem much less daunting.

The high expectations I have for myself will serve as a guidepost for my choices. And over time, I would develop the ability to make difficult revisions if necessary, growing more confident in my decision-making abilities along the way.

JONATHAN ZITTRAIN

Don't wait for an opportunity, create an opportunity.

I never expected a project that started in Michigan would lead to a meeting in Texas with a professor from Massachusetts that happened because of a conversation in California. But the world works in strange ways.

It all started when Jonathan Zittrain, an accomplished professor at Harvard Law School, came across a link to 52 Cups on a website and then mentioned the project on Twitter. I sent him a quick thank you for helping spread the word, and he said if I were ever in the Boston area we should get coffee.

A month later, long after the conversation had faded from memory, I was in San Francisco, visiting friends before traveling to the South by Southwest (SXSW) conference in Austin, Texas. I had met up with my friend Kelly, who mentioned her boss was speaking on a panel at SXSW. She told me to check it out because a guy named Jonathan Zittrain was on the panel and always gave a fascinating presentation.

I knew the name sounded familiar, but couldn't put my finger on the reason. After going back through my email archives, I put two and two together: it was the law professor from Twitter! I sent him a message, and a week later, Jonathan and I were sitting in the crowded Austin convention center, having a great conversation. What are the odds?

* * *

Kelly was right; Jonathan is fascinating. To kick off our conversation, Jonathan gave me a condensed history of the Internet (he wrote *The Future of the Internet—And How to Stop It*). Jonathan has a great ability to explain intricate concepts in an interesting manner. Plus, he has great stories.

My favorite was how he had gotten involved with the Internet back when only serious techies understood it. Although he was only 12, Jonathan had been intrigued with the Internet and had found a way to get online and join different communities where other technology geeks met (an activity his parents didn't know about until they received the hefty phone bill). Not wanting to reveal his age out of fear people wouldn't take him seriously, Jonathan made sure to be as articulate as possible to appear older. The strategy paid off. He was selected to be a moderator for an online forum, where he built a great reputation—he wasn't even 15.

The best part was when he explained how Texas Instruments (the forum to which he contributed) was going to be hosting a large convention and had asked him to be the keynote speaker. They had no idea how old he was, and he had decided not to tell them. Instead, he packed his bags, boarded a plane, and landed at the airport where a half dozen very surprised men welcomed him. Once they had gotten over the fact he was so young, the businessmen let him give the keynote. It was a big hit with conference attendees.

The mix of delight and nostalgia Jonathan showed as he continued telling stories from his life made our conversation delightful. Stories like the time he had met Stephen Colbert, or how he had gone to Yale to study Artificial Intelligence and ended up with a Law degree from Harvard.

He told me that he had stayed at his first job after law school for two and a half weeks before quitting. He had accepted a job in Washington, D.C., quickly realized he hated the job, and promptly quit. He didn't see any value in "sticking it out" for a year. In his mind, every day spent at the law firm was a missed opportunity to be working on a career he wanted.

As he later said, "Why settle for anything less than the life you truly want?"

He decided to head back to Harvard where he co-founded the Berkman Center for Internet & Society, which would later spin off Creative Commons, which encourages the free exchange of knowledge online. He was the first Executive Director of the center while also teaching first-year law classes at Harvard.

Although highly distinguished, Jonathan is down-to-earth. I thoroughly enjoyed his fresh perspective, wit, and insight on life. During the conversation, Jonathan brought up this idea of affordance. It is a term social scientists use to illustrate that at any one time, there is a set of actions we can perform—choices we can make. We all have them, but the number and degree of the choices vary with each person and change constantly.

For example, having five dollars in your pocket leads to a set of options. Having 50 dollars leads to a different set. How you choose to utilize your affordances determines how many more you will create. Accepting a job offer in New York will lead to a much-different outcome than accepting a position in Toledo. Deciding to go for a run after work will create a different outcome than meeting a friend for dinner, etc.

Past experiences, education, financial situation, and natural aptitude are just a few factors affecting affordances. However, some affordances are available to everyone. As Jonathan pointed out, Twitter, Facebook, and other online technologies have created new opportunities across the board.

It is a somewhat simple concept, but one that provoked my thinking. If each opportunity we take branches into a new set of opportunities, there are an exponential number of outcomes for the future. The potential is exciting, but you have to be willing to act on the opportunity.

Jonathan said that during his years of teaching, he found that many people, especially students, didn't realize the number of affordances—or opportunities—they had, or could create for themselves.

The opportunity to keynote a major conference hadn't come out of thin air; Jonathan had made that happen by making a name for himself doing something he loved. He had turned an affordance into an opportunity that fit his skill set—and that opportunity spiraled into many more.

That's what I took away from our conversation: everyone can create incredible opportunities for themselves. The lesson was not just a result of Jonathan's advice, but also of how the meeting came about in the first place.

I capitalized on three different affordances. I had made friends during an internship in San Francisco two summers earlier, which gave me a reason to visit San Francisco; I had started a blog, and I joined the student group going to SXSW—three very separate activities I never expected would bump into each other. But they did, and the result was a chance to meet Jonathan.

* * *

Discover what sparks your interest and dive into it headfirst; you never know where the path will lead, because the world works in strange ways.

MIKE WARDIAN

Mike's office in Washington, D.C.
Small brewed coffee

**Figure out what your goals are so you know where to
find the finish line.**

Mike Wardian is an ultra-marathon running junkie. He gets
up at dawn to run 12 miles before leaving for work. Then he
does another 12 miles during lunch. He completed 17 marathons in 2010, qualified for the Olympic trials twice, and is
preparing for a trip to South Africa for the Two Oceans
Marathon (about 34 miles) and the Comrades Marathon (56
miles), before running the Badwater 135 Mile race in Death
Valley a few months later. He is a fierce competitor on the
road and both respected and feared by other ultra-
marathoners.

However, that is not the Mike I met for coffee.

A basic Google search had led me to Mike. The Michigan
State Alumni Association highlighted his running accom-
plishments in an article, which led me to his personal website
where I discovered he was running the D.C. Marathon, which
was perfect as my friend Jess, and I were running the D.C.
Half-Marathon. When I reached out to him, I discovered he
lived in D.C., and we scheduled a coffee meeting on the day
before the race.

When I walked into his unassuming office, tucked away in a building off Wisconsin Ave. just outside of Washington, D.C., Mike greeted me before we sat down at a conference table adorned with a model cargo ship sitting in the middle. Aside from being sinewy like a seasoned runner and having long hair tied in a knot at the base of his neck, he was like any businessman I'd met. He was wearing a tie, and our conversation started off in a formal tone with direct answers.

This made sense considering his experience with post-race interviews. I asked him questions about his running and training, and told him stories about my own running experiences. I also explained how I had found him. My attempts to get back into running had gotten me thinking back to my serious days of cross-country, when discipline was a crucial piece of my running success. Finding that discipline after a long running hiatus had been a challenge, I decided to find an ultra-marathoner for coffee because I could think of few things requiring more discipline than running for 30 hours straight.

* * *

Mike was born in Morgantown, West Virginia and moved to Washington, D.C. in fourth grade. He left the area to go to college at Michigan State, which at the time had a Division I Lacrosse team. He competed for a few years but ended up leaving the team to pursue other interests. He had never been interested in running but joined a friend for a race and realized he had a talent for the sport and the competitive drive to become good at it.

While continuing to pursue marathons, he took a job back in D.C., where he had been for the past ten years working as a freight broker. It was a job he enjoyed, but, more importantly, one that afforded him the flexibility that his training demanded (while also allowing him to spend time with his wife and two young sons).

Running itself isn't hard; it's just putting one foot in front of the other. The hard part is continuing to put one foot in front of the other when it starts to hurt. I asked Mike how he did it, and his response made it obvious that running was in his DNA. He said he was always the first person ready to start running and the last one who wanted to stop. In fact, he would have ideally been running 150-200 miles a week, but time constraints wouldn't allow it.

I asked him how he could keep running when he was 60 miles into a 100-mile race. He said he would hit patches that were tough, but he would push through those moments by focusing on his race goals, while making sure to get enough food and water. Before long, he would cycle out of the rough spot and start to feel good again.

At the start of his career, people told Mike he could neither run a 100-mile race nor run three marathons in one month, nor be a competitive runner while holding down a job. But he had tried anyway because he figured that even if the skeptics were right, he would rather find out for himself instead of taking their word for it. So far, he had proven them wrong on all fronts and also had some incredible times in the process—literally and figuratively.

As he said, there will always be 50 people telling you why you can't do something (and they may tell you with the best of intentions) but if you listen to those people, you will never get anything done. *You* have to decide what's best for you, and then do it.

* * *

When we parted ways after our meeting, I couldn't help but think about how I hadn't seen the *real* Mike. He is a runner, but I had only seen him as a businessman. Moreover, I felt like we had only scratched the surface of his running and travel adventures. But when you are juggling family, a running career, and a job, time is of the essence. I didn't want to take any more of his time than I already had.

Luckily, I had my chance the following morning. Less than 30 minutes after I had finished running my 13.1 miles through the streets of D.C., Mike finished his 26.2 mile race, claiming his fifth D.C. Marathon victory in the last six years.

Jess and I waded through the frenetic crowd to the VIP Hospitality tent where we found Mike recovering with his wife and two sons. I called out his name, and he walked over, smiling. We didn't talk long; just long enough to share race-stories, meet his oldest son, and snap a picture, before parting ways. I headed for the Metro station, and he went for post-race interviews.

Leaving the race felt much better than leaving his office. This time, I felt like I'd gotten to see the *real* Mike in his element—celebrating another marathon victory with wife and kids. This image is how I would remember Cup 34.

As an athlete with a full-time job and family, Mike understands time. Whether he is running a race or living his life, the clock is always adding pressure. To be a successful runner requires efficiency of resources—making the best use of time and energy. Being a successful husband, father, and business-man on top of that required even more.

We all have limited time and energy. Mike doesn't waste any of it. He is a great example of someone with clearly de-fined goals and priorities, which led me to examine my goals and priorities. I realized there are plenty of people who will say you can't accomplish something, and countless distractions that will try to get in the way—but if you have a clear finish line in mind, you can overcome those barriers.

And have a great time celebrating your victory at the end.

STACY BOHRER

Skype call from East Lansing, Michigan to Chicago, Illinois
Regular brewed coffee

Your past does not have to define your future.

Stacy Bohrer cuts straight to the chase.

The advice I had received multiple times during my senior year was to decide what I was passionate about and turn that into a job. Stacy told me she knew what she was passionate about—but consciously decided she wasn't going to make it her job.

She told me this as I sat in front of my computer; headphones plugged in, coffee at my side. On two different occasions we had tried to coordinate a coffee meeting in Chicago, but our schedules never aligned. So we decided to video chat instead. After sorting out technical difficulties, our conversation got started when Stacy asked, "So, how does this meeting work?" I explained that we talked and then I wrote, pretty straightforward.

* * *

I found Stacy through my friend Christine. The two of them had met a year earlier while working at a small start-up in Chicago. Stacy had given Christine good advice over the past year, and Christine thought she would likely have good insights to pass along to me.

She was right. Stacy subscribed to the notion that if you don't wake up excited to go to work, you should find a new job.

I also subscribed to that notion, so I asked her about that right away. She was straightforward as she explained that she knows herself well enough to know when a job is making her unhappy, or doesn't fit well, and she isn't going to waste her time working there. Life is too short.

Stacy works as an Account Executive for an online media network, and clearly enjoys her job. This fact led me to the assumption that the job was directly in line with her passions. It surprised me when she said this was not the case—the first of many surprises in our conversation.

She said her true passion was helping victims of rape, raising awareness of the issue, and bringing justice to perpetrators. However, after becoming very involved in a volunteer organization associated with Chicago hospitals, she realized she couldn't emotionally separate her work from real life. In order to maintain balance, the best career fit would be a job she enjoyed in another industry, with a separate volunteer position with less emotional charge.

Then she explained why.

Stacy was raped during her freshman year at Ohio State University. Like most rape victims, she never expected it would happen to her, especially because the perpetrator was a student she'd known from high school. Afraid to speak out about the event, Stacy had kept it a secret—a secret that would slowly spiral her into a deep depression. Her 3.9 grade point average slipped to a measly 1.4. She stopped wearing makeup, and rarely left the house in anything but sweatpants. She came to resent her college and essentially everyone connected to it.

It was obvious Stacy was drowning in negative emotions. Fortunately, once she realized this, she found the courage to come out about the attack. She told the authorities, and within a few weeks, a half dozen other women had also spoken up—Stacy hadn't been the man's first or only victim.

After the attack, Stacy had spent sleepless nights studying the Constitution and other legal documents, researching how to bring justice to the situation—both to her assailant and to OSU for their poor response to her initial rape complaint. Her efforts were successful. In 2005, she received the Jeanne Clery Campus Safety Award for demonstrating incredible courage in seeking justice and in working to improve how OSU and other colleges responded to student-rape complaints.

When Stacy decided to tell people, her intention was to spread the word to help prevent it from happening to others. While she didn't tell me the details of the incident, she said I could find them online.

A press release from the Jeanne Clery Campus award explained it all. Her assailant pleaded guilty to "sexual imposition" in the fall of 2004, and a federal civil-rights lawsuit against OSU was pending over their failure to remove the assailant from campus until a year and a half after the assault was reported. Stacy had also gone public, writing an editorial that appeared in the *Campus Watch* newsletter along with being interviewed for a segment of *Dateline NBC* that shed light on the problems with how campuses deal with sexual assault.

Speaking out helped Stacy move on. She transferred to Kent State and moved to Chicago after graduation for a fresh start. She found a job she enjoyed, married an incredible man (to whom she refers to as "the luckiest man in the world"), and found a great passion for life. When I asked her if she still held resentment for the event, she told me that while the incident was a part of her past, it was not a part of her identity.

She had originally let the rape consume her, but she decided that she was not going to let it control her life anymore.

Bad memories do sneak up on her occasionally—especially on the anniversary of the incident—but she said when she looked back, she feels like she is seeing a completely different person. Today, she is so much stronger than the person she was when the rape happened.

Instead of letting the event destroy her life, Stacy chose to fight and overcome it.

During our conversation, Stacy paused before explaining that the experience had made her a better person. She paused because she didn't want the statement to sound like she was giving credit to the man who raped her. Finding the strength to speak up and move forward was what had made her a better person, along with the support of her therapist, husband, and family.

* * *

Our conversation continued and eventually drifted to other topics—mainly to how I was dealing with my impending graduation and the stress that came with it. Christine was right about Stacy; she left me feeling better about what the future held.

Stacy's story and insight put things into perspective. With the stress of life, it is easy to become consumed with how the future might unfold, but as Stacy told me repeatedly, I have to relax and trust that life will work out as it should.

And I believed her because her story shows that with the strength, power, and resilience of the human spirit, it is possible to make the future brighter than the past.

TOM IZZO

Michigan State University Basketball Offices in East Lansing, Michigan

No coffee, just conversation

Decide what you value, so you know what you're willing to pay to get it.

For fans of college basketball, and especially of Michigan State, Tom Izzo is a hero. As of 2011, he had led MSU's basketball team to the 2000 National Championship, six Final Fours and six Big Ten Championships. In 2011, he earned the prestigious Legends of Coaching Award. And, a year before, when the Cleveland Cavaliers made him an offer to coach in the NBA, the East Lansing community responded with a "We Love Izzo" ad campaign to show the coach how much they wanted him to stay, which he did.

But as I sat in his office, all of his prominence melted away. Tom is just a genuine guy from a small Michigan town, happy to take an hour out of his day to talk with a fellow Spartan.

* * *

After the numerous conversations I'd had during the previous nine months, I noticed a distinct trend: life rarely goes according to plan. No one I'd talked to was doing what they expected they'd be doing ten years before. I'd also observed that, with the right approach, life would take you to unexpected and incredible places.

It is a fascinating concept: your life will inevitably go places you can't begin to imagine. The closer I got to graduation, the more that thought was on my mind. So, out of curiosity, I posed the question to Tom: When you were two weeks away from graduating, where did you think life would take you?

As I had walked past the National Championship trophies in the lobby, through the hallway lined with photos of NBA greats like Magic Johnson and Steve Smith, I couldn't help but assume Tom hadn't foreseen this would be the culmination of his career path.

I was right. He earned an education degree and had always thought he would be teaching somewhere within the K12 system. When he graduated from Northern Michigan University, jumping into a classroom to teach didn't feel right, so he opted for grad school instead. He had played on the basketball team during his undergrad years, and when he started school again, he decided to become the basketball team's Graduate Assistant. With his love for basketball and strong competitive spirit, it was no surprise that Tom decided to be a teacher on the court instead of in the classroom.

I asked him at what point he realized he wasn't going to be a teacher and discovered that he might have a shot at coaching Division I basketball.

Tom told me he and his college roommate (and best friend since age 9), Steve Mariucci, had spent time kicking around fantasies about successful coaching careers—creating aspirations they knew were unrealistic, but worth dreaming about anyway. As he said to me, "I'm sure you've spent time thinking about what it'd be like to be a millionaire." In reality, he figured the likely outcome would be possibly getting a coaching gig at some Division II school. Tom had clearly exceeded that goal. (Steve Mariucci has too: he went on to coach for the San Francisco 49ers and Detroit Lions. Both coaches attribute their successes to the support and guidance they received from the other.)

While Tom wasn't downplaying his success as he told the story in retrospect, it seemed like the whole thing had been easy: Reaching an ambitious dream is hard enough, exceeding one is almost unthinkable. So I asked him what made the difference between coaching Division II and Division I. What separated good from great?

Tom didn't ponder the question; he knew the answer immediately: Sacrifice.

At age 29, Tom was working as a graduate assistant at Michigan State, making $4,000 a year, often working 18-hour days, with no girlfriend—because "what woman dates a man who makes $4,000 a year?" While his friends were working in stable jobs, establishing their careers and settling down with wives and kids, Tom was fielding an increasing number of calls from his mother inquiring when he was going to wise up and "get a real job."

It hadn't been an easy lifestyle, but he knew that it was what it would take to reach the next level. He said he had reached an incredible level of success because he'd been able to persist in moments where most people quit. His path involved great sacrifice. While Tom was proud of the program he had built and grateful for the opportunities he's had, his life had not been without regret. He juggles the demands of a stressful career with his role as a husband and father; he also looks back and knows there are many things he could have done differently. I appreciated Tom's honesty—he wanted me to recognize there were pros and cons to every career path.

Stress and pressure were the price Tom paid for a chance to cut down the net after earning a National Title, to dress up as a Spartan in front of 16,000 adoring fans, to watch young freshman players become confident graduates, and to have a lasting impression on a community and a university.

* * *

We had been talking for an hour when Tom's phone rang. He pretended he didn't hear it. When his secretary buzzed him to say he had someone waiting to talk, he said he'd be a second and then continued telling me stories—as if he had all the time in the world.

When we finally wrapped up our conversation, he said, "Well, I hope there was something helpful in that," and I assured him there was. Talking with Tom brought me an incredible sense of relief.

The truth is, for the past year, I'd had a quiet, yet relentless voice in my head creating an urgency to succeed. I am grateful for my internal drive, bit it had become a problem, a fear that if I don't "succeed" within a year or two of graduation, I will miss my window of opportunity and, more importantly, let a lot of people down.

I explained this to Tom, and he made it very clear my assumption was wrong. Success does not have a standard protocol or predetermined timeline. Some people fast track to success, but others take an indirect route. He told me not to worry about the expectations of others; what I expect from myself is a heck of a lot more important than what others expect from me.

Near the end of the meeting, Tom looked at me and said, "Decide what you value, so you know what you're willing to pay to get it. Then pursue that goal with discipline and a strong work ethic—but not to the point of obsession."

Because when the time was right, the hard work would pay off. Although, before I did that, I needed to decide what I was willing to sacrifice.

PEGGY BRANNAN

Motor City Brewing Works in Detroit, Michigan
Small French-pressed coffee

Be a part of something bigger than yourself; make a difference.

It was a sunny day when I visited the Green Garage in Detroit, and the hour-long drive was just what I had needed to clear my head from a stressful few weeks of school. When I arrived at the address, I found an old building clearly under construction, which I had to circle a few times to make sure it was the right spot.

I entered the building, carefully stepping into the large front room filled with construction equipment, and made my way around the corner where I found a few dozen people clustered around two large tables, positioned between various piles of building materials. The tables were covered with sack lunches brought from home, with baked goods for sharing sitting in the middle. I found Peggy Brennan and received a warm welcome before I was ushered to an open spot at the table and introduced to the crew.

A friend had suggested I meet with Peggy for coffee, but the simple meeting turned into an afternoon adventure. Together, Peggy and her husband Tom ran the Green Garage in Detroit, which was a venture that was not easily labeled. In

2008, Peggy and Tom bought the 90-year-old building, which in its glory days had been a showroom for Model T automobiles before becoming one of Detroit's numerous boarded-up buildings. The vision for the purchase was to restore the building (which was listed in the National Historic Registry) to its original condition and turn it into a resource center and co-working space for entrepreneurs starting environmentally sustainable businesses.

It began as an idea based on the triple-bottom-line business model, where the focus was not just profits, but also the environment and the community. The project had been the result of the efforts of 200 individuals working together to make a difference in Detroit's Midtown neighborhood.

Because it was a group effort, each Friday the Garage hosted a community lunch where anyone interested in the project could come and learn about how the project was progressing. Peggy suggested I join. That's how I ended up having lunch with people from ages four (kids of one of the main workers) to 74 (an older couple who had been longtime friends and supporters of both Peggy and the project). It certainly felt like a community and the laughter and light-heartedness of the lunch made me feel at home; there was an overwhelming sense of purpose and excitement about the renovation project, which had required much problem-solving and elbow grease.

When the meeting ended, Peggy took me on a tour of the building, and I was blown away by everything I saw. It was a net-zero renovation, which meant the project was trying to be as efficient as possible. Just about everything I saw was recycled, reused, or repurposed in one way or another.

* * *

After the tour, we headed across the street to Motor City Brewing Works, a restaurant with a vibrant young atmosphere that counteracted the doom-and-gloom picture the news paints for Detroit. We ordered a large French-press of coffee to share as I learned more about Peggy.

Not long after we started talking, Peggy's sister and two nieces joined us and our conversation drifted to Detroit's history. They were realistic about the problems facing the city, but were adamant that the city was filled with opportunity for those willing to get their hands dirty—people willing to start projects like the Green Garage.

They were so excited to be a part of the rebuilding efforts that I was surprised to find out their project had happened almost by accident.

After their three kids had grown, Peggy had started working on a Master's degree in Library Science while Tom worked as a consultant for Accenture. After 20 years in the business, Tom needed a change of pace and decided to retire—but he wanted a project to occupy his free time.

Some of their friends had developed an interest in sustainability, often testing new ways to save energy, lower costs, and reduce the negative impact on the environment in their homes. Peggy and Tom found themselves trying different things around the house and then getting together with their group of friends to swap stories. They were enjoying themselves in the process, and before long the group was holding weekly meetings. They hadn't planned for something big to emerge from the group, but the seed of an idea had been planted and, over the course of seven years, grew into the concept for the Green Garage.

Peggy and Tom started a real estate search that led them to the old historic building in Midtown, and they decided to buy it and turn their idea into a reality. Eighteen months later, they were ready to officially open the doors after completing the arduous, yet wonderful, renovation project.

I loved the story because it paralleled my life and hit home. Two years before, my friend Brett and I had started getting together for a beer every Friday to talk about ideas and collaborate on projects. We hadn't expected anything big to come out of the meetings, but we started inviting others until our group of three had turned to six, then twelve, and eventually a few dozen people contributing to an exciting entrepreneurial movement on campus.

What our group and the Green Garage shared was a sense of authenticity. People only joined if they were passionate enough to get their hands dirty, and it created a magical quality for the group. Everyone was excited to be a part of something greater than themselves.

It wasn't until I had crowded around a table of volunteers, happily spending their lunch break in an unfinished building in the company of like-minded individuals, that I realized how much belief in a vision could create meaning.

* * *

Whether we are conscious of it or not, we are all chasing meaning. We're all looking for proof that the ups and downs of life—the challenges, setbacks, and heartbreak—are worth something. We want to look back and know that our lives mattered, that we made a difference.

At times, the magnitude of changing the world can be daunting—to the point where there seems to be no sense in trying. The Green Garage and the efforts of all involved disprove that. Big change starts small. It takes one person with an idea and enough passion to attract others to join the cause. With time and continuous commitment, momentum builds, and positive change happens.

The Green Garage is one of many growing initiatives in Detroit, composed of passionate individuals pushing positive ideas forward.

But Cup 37 isn't just a story about Detroit.

It is a story about finding a community of people who fit your passion and aptitude, and allow you to contribute to something greater. It is a story about finding meaning, about making a difference.

It is a story for everyone.

SETH GODIN

Pain Quotidien in New York, New York
Small house coffee

Fail more often.

There is a passage in Seth Godin's best-selling book, *Poke the Box*, which goes like this: "Take action. Move forward. The world doesn't have room for standing still anymore. You have to innovate. Take initiative."

Take initiative.

Interestingly enough, that was how I ended up sitting across from Seth in a delightful French-style bakery in Manhattan, enjoying a fresh croissant with a dollop of organic chocolate spread, which Seth plopped on my plate and insisted I try because, "it puts Nutella to shame!"

I can replay the moment in my head like a movie: the atmosphere, the colors of the restaurant, the sound of the rain outside—and it's one I wouldn't soon forget. How could I forget the day I sat down with my hero (and 13-time *New York Times* best-selling author), for whom I had ridiculous respect and admiration?

* * *

The story starts five weeks before I met Seth. I was in Chicago, waiting for my connecting flight to Detroit after going to a wedding in Wyoming. Over the intercom, they announced the flight was oversold, and they were looking for volunteers to take a later flight. I raised my hand. Rerouting through Nashville and arriving in Detroit four hours behind schedule seemed like a small sacrifice to make in exchange for a $440 travel voucher to anywhere Southwest flew.

The real difficulty was deciding where to travel with my newly acquired funds. A mutual friend knew I was a big fan of Seth's work and said if I could get to New York City, he might be able to set up a meeting between the two of us. That was all I needed to hear. I sent some emails, booked a flight, and a few weeks later found myself sitting in front of Seth, which proved that his manifesto for taking initiative works.

I was excited to learn about the path that had led Seth to where he was today; however, our conversation took a different route. This detour shouldn't have surprised me. Seth was well-known for his unconventional thinking, so it made sense that our conversation would be unconventional as well. He wasn't interested in outlining his path to prominence—his recipe for becoming a successful entrepreneur, CEO, author, and game-changer.

The reason was that he, like every other success story, had a unique set of circumstances and skills with which to work. A set that neither I, nor anyone else, could replicate. I also had my own unique set of skills and circumstances. Thus, a more relevant use of our time would be talking about the *mindset* he had developed during the process. He wanted to help me identify places where his insight might be beneficial as I progressed in my career. I was moved—and grateful—for his genuine interest in helping me succeed.

The ironic part was that much of our conversation was about failure.

Seth told me he had failed a lot before he hit 30 and pointed out that I'd be well served if I got a few failures under my belt as well. He wasn't suggesting I set out to fail. He was suggesting that the best ideas and opportunities are the ones off the beaten path. Finding them requires taking calculated risks and being willing to push boundaries. Failure under the belt showed that you were striving for something.

His advice resonated with me because it was something the previous 37 conversations had helped me realize. When I started the 52 Cups project in July of 2010, I was a soon-to-be college senior, feeling the pressure of finding the perfect job by the time I graduated from college. I figured my first job was the first step of the rest of my life, and if I screwed up, I would let a lot of people down, and ultimately ruin my future. (It feels silly to write that now, but at the time, I believed it.)

Luckily, all these coffee conversations have shown me life isn't black and white; it is a changing shade of grey and a constant challenge to make the most of the opportunities it presents. Figuring life out requires failing a few times. And, with the right mindset and degree of perseverance, failure becomes an opportunity for growth instead of a scary dead end.

I had gone from fearing failure to accepting that I would fail at some point. Seth took the idea one step further. Not only did he tell me it was all right to fail, he encouraged it. He knows from his experiences that mistakes often breed incredible success. When you aren't afraid to fail, you open the doors to possibilities.

Failure often occurs where curiosity and courage collide. Something sparks your interest, and you find courage to explore a new idea. Then, it's tough to get something perfectly right on the first try, it doesn't succeed, or at least not the way you expected. You fall.

Then you pick yourself up and move forward, having learned something and grown in the process. You get to approach the same problem from a more-informed perspective. It's like learning to ride a bike. No one expects you to do it right on your very first try. You have to fall a couple of times in order to succeed. In fact, the faster you fall, the faster you learn—push a boundary, fail, learn, try a new route, and repeat.

Somewhere along the line, probably in grade school, failure became a bad thing, something to avoid at all cost. But, as Seth said, testing ideas and pushing boundaries—going through a hundred ideas that don't work—is the best way to find the one (remarkable) idea that does.

Unfortunately, knowing this doesn't make failure any easier. Seth told me, even after years of writing best sellers and running successful companies, he still feels the fear of failure. However, he has gotten better at recognizing when the fear is sneaking up on him, which helps him beat it.

Pushing boundaries is hard for everyone.

* * *

Looking back on the meeting, the advice Seth gave me sounded like a lot of work: fighting resistance, getting rejected, and learning from failure. But when I left our meeting, I was filled with incredible energy. Seth had given me a wonderful gift.

He gave me permission to get into trouble, make some mistakes, and get my hands dirty. He knew that curiosity and courage would lead to something great.

I believed him because it was curiosity and courage that had motivated me to volunteer to get off that plane and plan a spontaneous trip to New York City for a chance to meet someone I admired. I could have taken the comfortable route by staying in my seat and not raising my hand, but I would have missed out on an incredible experience.

Cup 38 and Seth's advice reaffirmed my actions and gave me the fuel necessary to keep starting projects, making a ruckus, taking risks, traveling, meeting people, asking questions—and ultimately looking for good ideas.

Of course, in the process, there will be failures. But if failures breed the best success, then may be I should be so scared after all.

COLIN WRIGHT

Kaffibarin in Reykjavik, Iceland
Americano

When you follow your passion, the future is always exciting.

During my first couple dozen Cups, I heard the same advice repeatedly: travel while you're young. I decided it was best to start taking some of the advice I had accrued. I had a bit of money in my savings account from working throughout college, so, after receiving my diploma, I packed my bags and set off for a five-week adventure through Europe, with plans to drink coffee along the way.

My first international coffee was with Colin Wright, a traveler I found through Twitter.

It happened while I was leaving Iceland's Blue Lagoon (a recommendation from Cup 21), where I enjoyed sitting in 100-degree water with freezing 30-mph winds blowing around me.

After soaking, I finished eating an Icelandic hot dog (topped with ketchup, sweet mustard, fried onion, raw onion and remolaði) before taking advantage of the free Wi-Fi at the resort.

Earlier, I'd sent out a tweet looking for someone in Reykjavik interested in having coffee and Colin responded. The power of social media never ceases to amaze me. His twitter bio explained he was an entrepreneur who moved to a new country every four months. I responded to his tweet; I knew we'd have plenty to talk about.

Five hours later, we were sitting at Kaffibarinn, a trendy spot Colin had picked. When I arrived, it was empty aside from a few locals—too early for a big crowd—but filled with personality; Reykjavik was a city with character.

A few minutes later Colin walked in, and I introduced myself before we got drinks (coffee for me, green tea for him); we found our way to a table toward the back and started our conversation.

* * *

Colin was born in San Francisco and his family had moved to Missouri when he was ten years old. His aspirations had been to go to college in New York, but he ultimately decided the better option was to attend the school in his backyard at Missouri State University.

He had an interest in graphic design and Missouri State had a fantastic program that would allow him to work alongside great designers from around the world. When he left with his degree in hand, he headed to Los Angeles to make a name for himself and quickly succeeded. He went from working in a boutique design shop to starting a studio that attracted big-name clients.

Colin had several career goals, but the biggest was to make enough money to quit his job and travel the world. By age 24, his dream was becoming a reality. Within a year and a half, he realized that he would achieve his financial goal and could begin traveling.

Then one day, it hit him: *Why wait a year and a half to start pursuing my dream?* He decided to find a way to make international travel happen as soon as possible.

His solution was a unique recipe of entrepreneurship, blogging, and straightforward resourcefulness. The companies he had started in LA were companies he could run from any location with a computer and Internet connection. However, he wanted his travels to be more than just doing the same work from exotic locations. He wanted his travel to have a purpose. He decided he would start a blog and turn the adventure into a project. The result was Exile Lifestyle, a blog covering insights gained from both work and travel experiences, along with the results of various lifestyle experiments conducted on the road. The best part was that every four months he would move to a new country determined by the votes of his readers. Since 2009, he had lived in Argentina, New Zealand, and Iceland.

Colin told me the two questions he got most often were: how he managed to keep relationships together since he was always moving, and whether it was hard to leave a place he had grown to love. Both questions had crossed my mind. Four months seemed like just enough time to make a few solid friends and start to feel at home in a place.

Surprisingly, the pattern of starting over hadn't bothered him. He said he didn't like to get complacent, so the constant moving kept him on his toes. He was very up-front with people—especially potential romantic partners—that he was only going to be around for four months. Plus, he could use the power of the Internet to stay in contact with the new friends he'd made. To explain his mentality for leaving the country, he used a Dr. Seuss quote: *Don't cry because it's over. Smile because it happened.*

While it was difficult to leave something great behind, achieving his goal necessitated leaving—Colin recognized that. He was in a long-term relationship with a woman he truly loved when he decided to travel. While Colin had realized he needed to travel, his girlfriend realized she wanted to make Seattle home. Early on in their relationship, they had agreed that they never wanted to hold the other person back from their dreams. They wanted the best for each other and decided that in four month's time, they would break up and start their separate adventures.

Not only did they plan their breakup, they decided to throw a break-up party. The idea was to get their closest friends together for one last hurrah, to celebrate the wonderful times instead of focusing on the sadness of splitting up. As hard as it was to say goodbye, both Colin and his girlfriend knew bigger things were on the horizon.

* * *

I think the story about the break-up party says a lot about Colin. He is an interesting character: ambitious, unconventional, and obviously not afraid to try new things. His work ethic, creativity, and big-picture thinking have helped him create the life of an international traveler and become an expert at transitions.

Our talk came at a perfect time for me.

I had just graduated from college, which ended an incredible chapter of my life. I'd moved out of East Lansing, a city that had been good to me, and in three- or four days, I would be leaving Iceland for another country—saying goodbye to the new friends I'd just made. In a few more weeks, my European adventure and nomadic lifestyle would likely be replaced with a stationary life of gainful employment.

That's a lot of endings. But from Colin's perspective, it is also a lot of beginnings—chances for change, growth, a new opportunity, and more.

That is the lesson I will take away from Cup 39: if you vehemently pursue things for which you are passionate, you always have something to which you can look forward. Being excited about what comes next makes it easier to let go of the past and focus on the future.

It also put experiences into perspective and helps you enjoy the present. Knowing that my conversation with Colin would eventually end—as would my time in Iceland—reminded me to enjoy each moment, so when the time came to say goodbye, I would have good memories to add to my collection, and could look forward to what the next country and conversation would bring.

40

JANINA PASIK

Janina's home outside of Warsaw, Poland
Small brewed coffee

Always be good to others.

As I sat on a train to Warsaw, I had no idea what I would find when I arrived.

Since we met for coffee in November, Piotr Pasik, Cup 17, and I had become good friends. When he found out I was going to be in Europe, he insisted I swing through Warsaw to visit his grandmother (whom he was home visiting). After two weeks of being in big cities surrounded by typical tourist attractions, a chance to get off the beaten path sounded wonderful. I rearranged my itinerary so I could stop by for a visit.

Piotr and his cousin picked me up from the train station, and we drove 40 minutes to Nowe Miasto—a town of 2,500 where a five-minute walk could get you from one side of town to the other.

When we arrived, Piotr's grandma, Janina, welcomed me with a big kiss on the cheek and a hug like only an experienced *babcia* (grandma) could give. She didn't speak English but the twinkle in her eyes and the way she kept smiling as she clutched my arm told me everything I needed to know—she was excited I had come for a visit.

I dropped my bags in the living room, and Piotr's cousin got me a glass of water while his grandma and aunt finished preparing lunch. It made an American Thanksgiving dinner look like a snack: tomato noodle soup, salad, cabbage with sausage, stuffed chicken, fried chicken, meatballs, pickled veggies *and* three kinds of homemade desert. It was an incredible meal that left me stuffed (I discovered that when an adorable grandma offers you food, no matter how full you are, it is impossible to say no).

Once lunch finished, Piotr took me on a tour of Nowe Miasto and explained the town's history and culture. It was fascinating to see Poland from a native's perspective and get a feel for what life had been like for Piotr's family. His stories inspired me to ask Piotr if he thought his grandma would be willing to be a part of my project.

As the sun was setting, we returned to the house, and Janina insisted she cook us something for dinner; before I knew it, I was once again sitting at a table filled with dishes of food. I told Janina two crepes would suffice, but she insisted I needed four (which I ate, because, again, it's impossible to tell a Polish grandma no).

Piotr explained my project to his grandmother, and she agreed to share her stories with me, which Piotr would translate. When dinner finished, we remained sitting around the table so we could talk. The night was getting late, so I decided to start with a direct question: "If you could give one piece of advice to young adults, what would it be?"

I had no idea how the conversation would go and realized I was holding my breath as Janina pondered the question for a moment before providing an answer. Piotr listened to his grandmother's response and then took a moment to collect his thoughts and translate: Be very friendly to others, do good things, help.

* * *

Janina was 86 years old, which meant she was 18 when the Germans invaded Poland at the start of WWII. The invasion, which would last five years, had spurred several resistance movements, which Janina had quickly joined. Her involvement duties had varied, but a common task was to walk 12 kilometers to a hidden location in the woods where she would pick up bottles containing messages to be delivered to the hospital. She never knew what the messages said, or why they were being delivered to the hospital, she was simply a messenger.

I asked if her parents had known about her involvement and she said yes; her father and cousin had also been a part of the movement. When I asked her what would have happened had she been caught, she paused for a solemn moment before taking her index finger and sliding it across her neck, indicating a fate I didn't need Piotr's translation to understand.

As the German invasion intensified, Janina's family was removed from their home and forced to move in with another family—seven people stuffed into a one-bedroom house while a war raged on in their backyard.

The family did their best to make the most of the situation until the Soviets helped liberate Poland in 1944, and then the war ended in '45. A year later, she met and married her husband, a young man who had spent nearly six years as a Polish prisoner-of-war. The young couple, wanting to get as far away from the pain and destruction that was left once the war ended, moved to the south of Poland to raise their children. A few years later, their daughter fell ill so Janina and her husband packed up their stuff and moved back to Nowe Miasto to be closer to family.

Although the war had ended, Janina's struggles had not: she still faced life under a new communist regime, lived in a city trying to rebuild after great destruction, and would lose her husband at the young age of 55 to cancer.

As I sat at the kitchen table listening to Janina's story, with a small candle providing light against the encroaching darkness of night, I was deeply moved. This wonderful old woman, not even five feet tall, had endured a life filled with continual hardship, yet still had a twinkle in her eye and warmth in her smile.

When she asked Piotr if I had any more questions, I had so many thoughts swirling through my head I couldn't formulate one. I could only have Piotr pass along the message that I was inspired by her incredible strength.

* * *

The following day I visited the Warsaw Uprising Museum to learn more about the many people involved in the resistance movement. It was an incredible museum, and I appreciated it even more after hearing Janina's firsthand account.

As I wandered through the pictures and artifacts representing the horror, suffering, and imprisonment of Poland's past, I tried putting myself in her shoes and imagining how she must have felt, but I couldn't. What Janina went through in her adolescence was far beyond what I could grasp. I reflected instead on her initial advice: "Be friendly to others, do good, help." The words seemed simple at the time, even cliché. But, after getting to know Janina, I learned that even those simple ideas could have powerful results.

When you are facing a truly dark situation, the best way to move forward might be to do whatever you can to bring light to others.

41

ROMAN KROKE

Art House Tacheles in Berlin, Germany
Espresso

Find balance; it makes life more interesting.

I was sitting on a small floor cushion inside a fourth-floor studio in Art House Tacheles. It was an art center in Berlin, Germany, which began as a department store in the Jewish quarter and later a Nazi prison. When the Berlin Wall fell, the partially demolished building was taken over by artists and transformed into studio space and a nightclub. Its interior is filled with wall-to-wall graffiti and a stream of visitors looking at both the building and the art of its tenants.

Roman Kroke's studio was much calmer than the rest of the building. Old American music played softly in the background while small candles on the table created a soft light illuminating the walls—walls covered with black and white photos, old handwritten notes, and illustrations depicting scenes from the 1940s. After spending a day discovering Berlin's history, I was moved to be in a building—and room—with such history and character.

The illustrations on Roman's wall depicted excerpts from *Diaries of the Dutch Jew Etty Hillesum.* It was one of his most prominent projects. Etty was in her mid-20s during the Holocaust. The book, published posthumously, started with intimate diary reflections describing the difficulties of life in Amsterdam during the German Occupation. The second half was a series of letters she sent from the Westerbork concentration camp, where she lived until she was taken to Auschwitz and killed. Roman had illustrated several scenes from the book for a documentary titled *The Convoy* and was turning the illustrations into a published book.

The pictures and letters covering Roman's walls served as both research and inspiration. His work focuses on the Holocaust and Berlin's history, which helps draw attention to events that are too often forgotten or misinterpreted. He loves interpreting history from a fresh perspective.

As he told me, "The events of yesterday can teach us lessons we can apply tomorrow."

Roman's career was much different than the one he had when he left law school. As a young student, he had a difficult time narrowing his many interests into one degree, but eventually settled on International Human Rights Law. After several internships, his law career got off to a good start; however, he quickly realized he was not meant for the life of a lawyer. His true passion was illustration.

He continued working part-time as a lawyer and researcher while he launched his art career. Eventually, he reached a point where he could be an artist full time. When I asked Roman if there was something he wished he had known back when he finished earning his law degree, he answered with a metaphor: "Every tree begins as a seed and grows inch by inch. No seed becomes a big tree overnight, because every step is necessary."

It was a powerful way of explaining you have to endure both good and bad to grow.

Roman answered many of my questions with the same poetic insight—or simply answered my question with one of his own. I appreciated his insight and imagination; it kept me on my toes.

Roman sees the world from a unique perspective. This quality led to fascinating and thought-provoking conversation. I could see why the friend with whom I was staying in Berlin had suggested we meet. Our conversation covered a variety of topics: one minute we were talking about the art workshops he ran for high school kids, the next I was writing down a list of my favorite country-music artists.

I had told him I liked country music because it reminded me of home, and he asked me to write down a few names, as he'd never been a country listener. After I had written the list, Roman looked at it and commented that my handwriting was interesting: very linear—straight lines, sharp points, and few

curves. I found his observation intriguing, because earlier that week I looked through the dozens of photos I had taken since I started my trip and realized I was drawn to images that had straight lines and symmetry. I took out my camera and showed him one of my favorites: a cross-section of the Berlin wall that had several straight, parallel, lines.

Roman looked at the photo and agreed that it was very linear, but then he noted the fluffy clouds and blue sky were an important piece of the photo. He said without the sunny backdrop, the image would be too structured and therefore boring. Then he pointed out how the reverse was also true: an image of a blue sky without substance would also be boring.

What made the photo interesting was the mix of the two: the dichotomy of the wall's strong presence against the peacefulness of the sky. It had the right balance.

I loved his critique of my photo because his insight related to more than just photography: It related to life. "The key is finding the right balance."

Then Roman and I talked about the challenges of doing creative work, especially when self-employed. It was clear many of his challenges stemmed from finding the right mix of two things: working hard without burning out; moving a project forward without forcing it; enjoying the moment, but still preparing for the future; being creative yet pragmatic, confident yet humble. The list continued.

* * *

I was glad I had met Roman and heard his stories before going back to the U.S. and jumping into a career. Too often, people get wrapped up in their work and neglect other aspects of their lives: family, friends, health, etc. It works for a while, but if the balance is off for too long, things start to fall apart.

Cup 41 and the picture of Berlin serve as a reminder that life needs structure, but not so much that it doesn't have blue skies too.

Mihaela Fabian

Museon Museum in Den Haag, The Netherlands
Café Americano

Raise the potential of others.

Before Cup 42, I had never given Romania much thought. After Cup 42, I decided I needed to visit Romania, so I immediately planned a visit later in my travels through Europe.

Here's a very quick history lesson: After WWI, Romania was experiencing an era of prosperity. At the start of WWII the country wanted to remain neutral; however, a Soviet ultimatum forced them to the Axis side. Then, when the war ended, the Soviet Union forced Romania into a social republic. Over the following decades, the Communist government established a reign of terror over the country.

In 1974, Nicolae Ceausescu took over as the Romanian President and began borrowing heavily to finance economic programs for the Socialist Republic of Romania. This left the country more than $13 billion dollars in debt. To solve the problem, Ceausescu began exporting agricultural and industrial products to repay the debt to other countries. The plan worked economically but left Romanians in a dire situation: Ceausescu's exports depleted the country of adequate resources to survive; Romanians faced food rationing and frequent electricity blackouts.

Mihaela Fabian was one of the many Romanians forced to endure the suffering and decline in the standard of living.

* * *

We were sitting in the cafeteria at the Museon Museum of Popular Science in Den Haag (near Amsterdam) as Mihaela recounted her experience. As a young woman in school, she would often do her homework in the dark during power outages and often ran out of common food staples. Mihaela shared a vivid memory of the first time she was able to leave Romania. The train station where she arrived had bananas and beer for sale—she let out a cry of joy she was so excited. There were no bananas or beer in Romania.

It was clear her upbringing hadn't been easy, but she said close family ties helped her through it. Luckily, life was very different now. The Romanian Revolution of 1989 brought an end to Ceausescu's dreadful reign and paved the way for democracy that was slowly rebuilding the country from its rocky past.

As for Mihaela, she was no longer a young woman facing food shortages in Romania. She was now the wife of the Romanian Ambassador to the Netherlands.

* * *

My aunt Kim met Mihaela through the International Wives Club she had joined when my uncle's job moved them from Houston, Texas to the Netherlands. The club, which had a couple dozen ladies from all different countries and cultures, helped women who were new to the country meet other women in the same situation. When my aunt told me about the group, she mentioned Mihaela would be fascinating to talk with.

As luck would have it, one night while out to dinner, we ran into Mihaela, who was having dinner with a friend. My aunt introduced us and we set up a meeting for the following morning.

* * *

I was fortunate to grow up in a household where we never worried if there would be enough food on the table or if the lights would work when we flipped the switch. This made it difficult to grasp what Mihaela's life had been like growing up. It was even harder to comprehend how a ruler could allow his people to suffer in such a way (especially when, a week later, I visited Bucharest, and saw the multi-billion-dollar parliament building Ceausescu had built during his reign).

I asked Mihaela if, during those difficult times, she had ever imagined she would be leading the distinguished life of a diplomat's wife. She said she hadn't.

Then she told me a story of an older woman once telling her she was lucky. However, Mihaela's perspective was, "you pay a price for luck."

The best things in life don't come easy. Mihaela endured difficult times, worked hard and made sacrifices to get to where she is today. In college, Mihaela studied psychology before becoming a speech pathologist for children with hearing impairments. There was great joy in her voice as she described years spent working with kids—watching their growth and development.

She explained that the woman she had been with when we saw her the previous night was a former student of hers. The young woman had lost her hearing when she was six months old because of an incorrect dose of antibiotics. This left her facing an uncertain future. Fortunately, Mihaela had found her, and through their work together, the girl developed the necessary skills to excel in high school and continue on to college, where she was now working on an advanced degree in medicine.

Mihaela was filled with pride as she told the story. She said she stayed in touch with many of her students, and it was obvious she had been good at her job.

However, when her husband became an ambassador, Mihaela knew she would have to quit her work to help serve her country.

She clearly missed it. While we were talking, two dozen preschoolers on a field trip ran past us toward the museum entrance, instantly stealing Mihaela's attention in the process. She really loved kids.

But she also loved her country. Despite the difficulties of its past, Mihaela spoke of Romania with great affection, and was grateful for the opportunity to show others what the country has to offer. She spends a lot of time meeting people and talking about Romania, which—between her warm personality and easy sense of humor—is a role that suits her well. It didn't surprise me when she said she made friends wherever she went.

In fact, it was when were on the topic of friendships when she casually said, "We have to raise the potential of others."

That's the statement that stuck with me after Mihaela and I ended our conversation. I understood then what drove her to become what she is today. Whether it is helping young patients, serving as a diplomat for Romania, or befriending a Texan recently transplanted to the Netherlands, Mihaela sees the potential in others, and that's what gave her own life meaning.

43

Yasmina Boustani &

Katharina Schmitt

A local café in Cannes, France
Café Americano

It's the extra step that creates the opportunity.

On Friday, June 20th, at 8:30 PM, I sent Yasmina Boustani a Facebook message. At 9:10 PM she responded. By 9:41 PM that night we had arranged to meet for coffee the following morning.

* * *

It was because of a Facebook message that I was in France in the first place. A few weeks before I left for Europe, I received an unexpected Facebook message from my friend Trista, a recent alumna of Michigan State, who had moved to Texas. She knew I was headed to Europe and wanted to let me know she was going to be in Rome assisting with a study abroad program. If I could get to Rome, she would love to give me a grand tour of the city.

I told her I'd love to meet up and would contact her when I knew the dates I'd be in Italy.

When I emailed her the dates of my arrival, I discovered she would be spending that weekend in Cannes, France at the

Cannes Lion International Festival of Creativity. A few months earlier Bill Ward, Cup 9, and I were catching up over another cup of coffee, and he mentioned that if I were ever in France, it would be worthwhile to swing by Cannes to check out the festival.

I decided to reroute to Cannes and met up with Trista, hoping to find a big-hitter in the advertising industry to meet for coffee.

It was a great plan, but, like many of the plans I'd made during my trip, it took an unexpected turn. The last festival session I attended was the Future Lions Competition award ceremony. It is the culmination of a global competition where college students, working in teams of two, are challenged to "advertise a product from a global brand in a way that couldn't have been conceived five years ago."

There were over 800 entries submitted from around the globe, of which four finalists were chosen to attend Cannes.

Each of the finalists showed a short video explaining their concept, and it was fascinating to see the quality of the presentations and the innovation of the ideas. The first two were impressive, but it was the third idea, created by Yasmina and Katharina Schmitt, which struck me.

Their idea for 1-800 Flowers was to take the digital act of saying "Happy Birthday" on Facebook and make it more tangible, more meaningful. Their product, Flowers for Facebook, printed a person's Facebook birthday wishes on paper and used it to deliver a surprise bouquet of flowers to the birthday girl. It was a fun product with a very compelling video.

At the end of the presentation, the lively emcee put up the contact information and encouraged conference attendees to reach out to these talented young advertisers, stating very simply, "Hire them before they steal your job."

That's when I decided I wanted to talk to Yasmina and Katharina. Not only did I love their idea, I thought it would be more fun to talk to the future industry big hitters rather than the current ones.

* * *

So there we were, Yasmina, Katharina and me, sitting at an outdoor cafe a block from the Mediterranean Sea.

After we had ordered our coffee, we started getting to know each other better. Yasmina was originally from Beirut, Lebanon. She had earned a degree in Advertising and Art Direction from the Lebanese Academy of Fine Arts before enrolling at the Miami Ad School in Europe. That was where she met Katharina.

Katharina was from Mannheim, Germany. Her aspiration was to become a dancer, but she realized en route that she had a passion for advertising. She shifted her efforts toward a Bachelors degree in Economics and Marketing, before enrolling at the Ad School.

Katharina and Yasmina quickly became friends, then project partners, and then roommates in New York City, where they studied abroad for a semester. While there, they created Flowers for Facebook for a class project. Their professor encouraged them to submit the idea to Future Lions. They didn't think the idea was ready for Cannes, but followed the professor's advice anyway.

After a few tweaks, they submitted the idea and waited for a response, not expecting much. With so many submissions, they figured they didn't stand a chance.

They were happily wrong. The idea was good enough to make it to the final round. This meant Yasmina and Katharina were headed to France for an intense week of advertising adventures and one last hurrah together before Katharina headed to Germany to begin her first job and Yasmina returned to New York for one last semester.

They were loving their time at Cannes, reconnecting with old friends they knew from school who had since moved to different corners of the world. After going all the way to France to connect with friends from my backyard in Michigan, I could relate.

And it wasn't just France; along each step of my European adventure, I connected with friends: a running buddy from home now living in Poland, as well as former MSU classmates working in Scotland, Prague, and Poland.

It felt pretty surreal that an American, a Lebanese, and a German would all enjoy a great cup of coffee and conversation together in a cafe in France.

But at the same time, it felt perfectly natural. Technology is changing the way we connect and do business—global collaboration is becoming as easy as collaborating with the cubicle (or, in my case, the table in a coffee shop) next door. It is an incredible opportunity, but only for those willing to leverage technology—those willing to take action, take risks and think globally.

It doesn't happen while sitting at home behind a computer. It happens when you get outside your comfort zone, find ways to travel and try new things. I made two new friends because Yasmina and Katharina were willing to enter a competition they had a slim chance of winning, and were willing to say yes to a Friday-night Facebook message from a stranger asking to meet for coffee.

It is easy to take two seconds and write "Happy Birthday" on a friend's Facebook wall. It's a little harder to take an extra step and do something memorable. But if Cup 43 taught me anything, it is this: it's the extra step that creates the opportunities.

And in today's world, those opportunities can literally take you around the world.

TONY STONE

Stoats Porridge Oat Bar Headquarters in Edinburgh, Scotland
Office-brewed coffee

It's important to have a plan, but the real key is having the courage to take the first step.

Don't be afraid to change directions. This was the mentality I had going into my European adventure, and the reason I ended up in Scotland.

My flight back to the States was out of London, so I decided that's where I would spend the last four days of my trip. However, when a friend from Michigan State emailed me to say she was going to be in Scotland for the TED Global conference, I decided to revise my plan. I'd spend two days in Edinburgh before taking a short train ride to London for my last two days.

* * *

I was weary from travel when I rolled into Scotland at 10:30 pm, but the beauty of the castle-lined landscape resting under a crescent moon restored my energy. After pausing to take a few photos and drink in the moment, I headed toward the hostel I'd booked, making a quick stop inside a convenience store along the way for a late-night snack.

It was the bold green packaging on the Stoats Porridge Oat Bar that caught my attention.

After looking at the package, I discovered it was produced locally in Edinburgh. And after eating the bar I checked online to see if the bars were available in the States. The search naturally led me to the Stoats website, where I read about the offbeat origins of the company. It was a fascinating story (filled with delightful British vernacular), so the next morning I decided to email the company to see if I could grab a coffee with co-founder Tony Stone. He agreed, and we set up a meeting.

* * *

When I arrived at the Stoats headquarters in the outskirts of the city, I wasn't sure I was in the right spot. But then I noticed the small white Stoats sign, on a door nestled among a handful of larger manufacturing shops. I cautiously turned the handle and walked inside to find a simple setting: large bags of raw oats, stacks of cardboard boxes, and various flyers on the walls. Basically, I saw what you would expect from a manufacturing plant if you spent any time imagining what a manufacturing plant might look like.

Tony heard me enter, and yelled hello from his office down the hallway before coming out to meet me. He was tall, lanky, and personable, with a relaxed disposition and friendly Scottish accent. We walked into the office he shared with two other employees. He apologized for the disorder—piles of promotional material and files lined his desk, random boxes of product samples strewn about—and the lack of quality coffee.

I told him I didn't mind; after seven weeks on the road, I was used to disorder.

* * *

Tony had always entertained the idea of starting a company, but he wasn't sure in what capacity. That changed the day he and his friend Bob went to a music festival. I like how their website explains it:

> Stoats began with an idea in 2004 to serve fresh porridge at music festivals. We listened to our mates moan and groan about what they had to eat to survive at music festivals. We knew that porridge would make a healthy, filling and tasty eating option, so we decided porridge was the future (and quite a cool way to spend the summer). Bob and Tony got a shiny wee mobile porridge bar and started selling freshly made porridge across the UK, and festival audiences loved it (and still do—look for the biggest queue at breakfast and you've found Stoats Porridge).

In 2004, porridge was getting a lot of attention in the press—it was one of Scotland's best exports and was an especially trendy food at the time. Tony and Bob saw an opportunity and decided to capitalize on it.

They decided to take it one step further: they would set up a small store where they'd sell porridge year-round. But reality intervened. When they approached the bank for a loan, they weren't able to get as much money as they requested.

But that didn't stop them; they just reevaluated the plan and decided to stick with selling bowls of fresh porridge to festivalgoers, advertising their product with a big banner alongside the truck that read:

STOATS PORRIDGE BAR

Their decision worked, business was booming, and (although they didn't see it) was about to change directions again.

Many of their customers misunderstood what "PORRIDGE BAR" meant. While the banner implied the type of bar synonymous with buffet, table, counter, etc., many concert goers thought that Stoats sold bars of porridge—like granola bars. The thought never occurred to Tony and Bob, but they figured if that's what their customers wanted, that's what they should sell. After a little experimenting in the kitchen, the original Stoats Porridge Bar was born and became an instant hit.

While hearing Tony's firsthand account of the company's growth, it became clear to me that it was their ability to be flexible and their willingness to try new things that allowed them to develop a successful business, one that continued to grow. It was a lot like my European trip: I had an itinerary, but it hadn't been so concrete I couldn't revise it when a better opportunity arose.

Changing directions can be scary, especially if you have taken a lot of time devising the original plan. But the thing is, you can't predict life. If you think you have total control over your plan, you're setting yourself up for failure because something unexpected will inevitably occur.

However, if you accept that life will throw you curveballs (both good and bad), the unexpected moments can turn into the greatest opportunities. Had Tony and Bob been dead-set on sticking to the plan, the lack of funding from the bank could have completely derailed them. Or they could have ignored their customers and neglected the opportunity to take their business in a new, and better, direction.

When I asked Tony what the greatest lesson he'd learned in the past five years was, he told me this: "Start small."

He said, oftentimes, the idea you are most excited about ends up going nowhere while an offshoot of the idea becomes an unexpected hit. That is why they roll out new products in small test batches; if it works, they roll it out to the whole market.

Starting small allows them to take smart risks. Take enough small risks, and you can start to see big change. It's a smart strategy, much better than devising a grand scheme and then aborting it at the first sign it won't work.

* * *

I was thinking about my conversation with Tony while walking back to the hostel from the Stoats Headquarters.

A year ago I hadn't planned to be drinking coffee in Europe. I'd just wanted to meet new people in the city where I lived, so took a risk and invited a stranger to coffee. It worked, so I kept at it; one thing led to another, and I ended up in Scotland surrounded by beautiful scenery and wonderful people—and drinking coffee with strangers.

While it is important to plan ahead, success does not require some big, elaborate scheme. It requires the courage to take that first step. And then another. And then another.

If you can do that, life will take you to incredible—and deliciously unexpected—places.

STEVE WOZNIAK

Marie Calendar's in Los Gatos, California
Water over lunch

Talent is overrated; it's practice that's important.

This story begins nine months before our meeting happened. Around Cup 16, I was talking about 52 Cups with Todd, a friend at work, when an idea hit him, "You should try to set up a meeting with Woz, the co-founder of Apple! I know he'd do it—in fact, I bet he'd even fly to Michigan."

I figured I had nothing to lose, so I explored ways to contact him. I searched his website, tried Facebook, asked a few friends. Nothing worked. My last resort was to search "Steve Wozniak" on anywho.com. I called the phone number, only to reach Steve Wozniak the pro fishing reporter, not Steve Wozniak the computer genius. I decided that it just wasn't meant to be and moved on.

Then March rolled around, and one day I woke up to this email from a good friend at Michigan State: FYI, Steve Wozniak will be the June commencement speaker. I bet we could get a coffee date set for you.

A strange feeling washed over me. Todd had been right; Steve Wozniak was flying to Michigan. And there was a chance we could have coffee.

The day of graduation, I found a way to get invited to a reception where he was speaking, (and stood next to him while drinking a cup of coffee—but that doesn't count). He was fascinating to talk with and very approachable, so I explained my project and invited him for coffee. He said he'd love to, but would have to take a rain check; he was headed to Detroit to watch a hockey game before his flight back to California. He gave me his business card and told me to email him sometime.

So I did. I sent him an email from Budapest, to let him know I was planning a trip to San Francisco to visit friends in July, and would love to meet up if he were around. A half-dozen email exchanges and a couple of flights later, I was riding my friend's green beach-cruiser bike down the sunny, tree-lined, streets of Palo Alto to meet Woz and his wife for lunch.

* * *

It was a fantastic lunch, culminating with a piece of wisdom that emerged when I asked him how he and his family had stayed grounded amid the fame and success. His advice, "Be true to yourself. Find out who you are and what you value—then don't let anything deter you."

For as long as Woz could remember, he had wanted to design computers. In high school, in college, in his first year working, Woz was designing computers during every spare moment. During his first year at Hewlett Packard, he designed the revolutionary Apple I and Apple II computers during nights and weekends away from work.

Woz knew he was been born to build computers—not because he wanted to make a million dollars or start a revolutionary new company, but because nothing brought him greater joy than solving complex computer problems. After he designed the Apple I, he actually gave away the designs to anyone who wanted them.

When he designed the Apple II, he was planning on doing the same thing, until Steve Jobs approached him about starting a company to commercialize the computer. At first, Woz said no. He didn't want to be a businessman; he wanted to be an electronics engineer. At the time, Hewlett Packard was the most prestigious place for engineers, so Woz saw no reason to leave.

But Jobs was insistent. He eventually won over Woz and they went on to found a company that revolutionized home computers and changed the future of technology forever.

Of course, it was much more complicated than that, but the bottom line is that Woz helped create a company that most entrepreneurs could only dream about building.

Then he walked away from it.

One reason was that a near-fatal plane crash left him with retrograde amnesia. He had no recollection of the crash, and also struggled with day-to-day short-term memory (although he did eventually restore his memory). The other reason was that he wanted to finish the college degree he'd abandoned when he went to start Apple.

What happened next was surprising. He became a teacher, to fifth-grade kids. It was an atypical move, but Woz isn't typical. He knows himself well enough to trust his decisions, even when they seem crazy to the outside world.

That's what impressed me most about Woz. More than his fame, his genius, and the fact that he had co-founded one of my favorite brands—it was his self-awareness (and self-assurance) that impressed me.

To know exactly who you are—and accept who you are—is a rare quality.

Sitting down with Woz and hearing him talk so candidly, and in such a genuine and humble manor, was refreshing.

Woz wasn't born with his computer talent. His expertise had been a gradual progression that developed because he was passionate and willing to work at the skill tirelessly.

That is the most important takeaway from Cup 45: Most people aren't born with remarkable talent.

While it's undeniable that Woz had an aptitude for computers, it was the hours, and hours, and hours of dedicated practice that gave him the ability to revolutionize the computer world.

If he hadn't been devoted to the craft, his skills would have been wasted.

Regardless of what your skills are and where you start, you can always get better. The people who are leaders in their field didn't start at the top; they worked their way there. I'm not saying natural aptitude isn't important; it is, just probably not as important as you think. Woz is a fantastic public speaker. His keynote at Michigan State's graduation was a great blend of information, inspiration, and entertainment. That's why he is invited to speak at events around the world—and why you would assume Woz had a natural aptitude for public speaking.

That couldn't be further from the truth. Growing up, Woz was so shy he wouldn't raise his hand in class or talk to the other kids in his computer club. He feared public speaking. But as the co-founder of Apple, he had people wanting to hear him speak, so he had to face his fear of public speaking. With devotion and practice, he developed a talent he never knew he had.

I understand this is a difficult idea for most people to believe. It is much easier to convince yourself that you just don't have the right kind or amount of talent, rather than accept the scary idea that success is attainable, just with a lot of hard work. It's easier sometimes to give up than to grow. I know this, because I have done it many times.

But Woz showed me how wrong I was to assume that talent has to be innate—he took away my excuse. Now I couldn't take the easy way out and blame my lack of talent. I would have to put in the hard work to develop talent.

BO FISHBACK

A local coffee shop in Kansas City, Missouri
Small brewed coffee

You have more potential than you think.

Bo Fishback was the self-proclaimed luckiest man in the world. By age 30, he had found his dream job. He worked as the president of Kauffman Labs for Enterprise Creation in Kansas City, Missouri, where his main task was allocating 100 million dollars a year to various entrepreneurial projects. It was a job that was easy to love, and one he saw himself doing for another 20 years.

Then, one Monday in February, he walked into work and announced his resignation—effective immediately.

The news came as a shock to Kauffman. It probably came as a shock to Bo as well—when he left work on Friday he had every intention of returning the following Monday. But life intervened.

At the insistence of his good friend, Eric Koester, Bo had gone to Los Angeles, where he competed in a 54-hour Startup Weekend Event. He pitched an idea that had been rolling around the back of his mind for a while. It was a last-minute decision to compete, and the decision paid off: not only did Bo's team win; they had attracted the attention of investors (including Ashton Kutcher), and raised nearly a million dollars overnight.

He explained this as we sat sipping coffee at the coffee shop in Kansas City, a five-minute walk from the headquarters of Zaarly—one of the fastest-growing, most-talked about start-ups of 2012. In just seven months, they had scaled their product, assembled a dynamic team, and left a noticeable impact on cities nationwide.

* * *

Bo had always known he would start a company. When he was four years old, Bo's father left his job at a hospital to start his own company, selling respiratory therapy supplies. When Bo was 18, his father sold his company and retired comfortably. Watching his dad run a business instilled the entrepreneurial bug in both Bo and his brother, who was also a successful entrepreneur.

However, at age 18, Bo didn't expect to be in the position he was in today. He'd grown up in a small Georgia town, where he drove 50 miles to and from school. By the time senior year rolled around, his top concern was finding a school outside of Georgia, where he could play basketball (he's 6'8"), and meet girls. He ended up at Southern Methodist University, and while his basketball career was short-lived, it was where he met his wife (and now mother of their newborn baby boy).

After earning a degree in Medical Biosystems, he went to work for a corporation that gave him a budget and said, "go start a new branch for our company." You could say he met their expectations. By the time he left, the team he'd built had over 200 employees. He then started his own company that (in what he calls a complete stroke of luck) sold within eight months. Next, he decided to pursue an MBA and headed to Harvard Business School, where he once again rolled out a successful venture. That's how he garnered the attention of Kauffman and landed a job helping other start-ups.

His motive for serial start-ups was simple: "I just like to build shit."

And he also got lucky: "I've had so many experiences where luck was on my side, I've reached a point where I just assume I'll be lucky."

Of course, the harder you work, the luckier you get. And Bo worked hard.

You wouldn't know it if you met him, though; he's easy-going, with a propensity for fun. He's also charismatic, optimistic, and visionary. In all honestly, after Bo took time out of his busy schedule to sit down and have a genuine conversation with me, I could have been convinced to relocate my life to Kansas City and join his team.

I wouldn't have been the first Michigan State kid to do it. Zaarly worked its magic on three of my closest friends (which was why I was visiting Kansas City in the first place). Bo could provide a chance to create something meaningful, and it was a hard offer to turn down.

It was a big vision and Bo thought it was going to work. But, even if it didn't, it would have been an incredible ride, an exciting chapter of life he could look back on as a reminder that he was willing to take a risk to create something great.

* * *

I will take a lot away from Cup 46, but what I will remember most is Bo's optimism and vision.

Everyone is capable of finding that once-in-a-lifetime idea or opportunity that captures their heart and changes their life (and the lives of others)—that risky idea that somehow doesn't seem risky at all. It is an idea you can't get off your mind, one that creates meaning and purpose.

But sadly, not everyone knows they have this capability.

Bo said he was lucky, but it took more than luck to stumble into a dream job (twice). I asked him what made him different from those who don't find meaningful jobs.

His answer was simple: "I surround myself with good people."

Cup 46 is a testament to the fact that a life filled with meaning, laughter, love, and fun is possible for everyone. It takes a lot of work to make it happen, but it is possible. If you don't believe that, surround yourself with people who do. Their contagious optimism and support will help lead you in the right direction.

Then when you find it (and don't settle until you do), reach out and help someone else, whether it's being a mentor to a young college student or a co-founder for a company that starts a movement.

Or better yet, do both.

BRITTANY FOX

A Skype call from East Lansing, Michigan to Bangkok, Thailand
Home-brewed coffee

If you never try, you will never know what is possible.

Brittany Fox had traveled to a lot of cool places.

However, in all of her travels, she never found a city to which she could envision herself moving. She liked Michigan, and that was where she wanted to stay.

Until she went to Thailand.

An interest in humanitarian work led her to a summer study abroad program spent volunteering in several different countries. When Brittany arrived in Pattaya, Thailand, she felt something she had never felt during her previous travels: a sense of connectedness. A thought from out of nowhere entered her head, "*I could live here.*"

A few years later, she made it happen.

Brittany relayed her story to me via Skype from her apartment in Bangkok, while preparing for a full day of work. I listened from my kitchen table in Michigan, relaxing before heading to bed. I had found her through a friend and was grateful technology made our conversation possible. The Internet connection wasn't ideal, but it held up long enough to hear her story.

* * *

During her first visit to Thailand, Brittany was volunteering with YWAM Thailand, a center that provides help, healing, and hope for women caught in Thailand's large prostitution industry. According to their website, Pattaya was known as Thailand's number-one sex destination. It was home to 20,000 male, female, and child prostitutes, who attracted over one million visitors each year.

Many of the women Brittany worked with shared the same heart-breaking story—they were single mothers facing the challenge of raising their children, while taking care of their aging parents. As the financial pressures increased, they felt powerless and saw no option other than prostitution.

YWAM worked to help these young women by providing them with an education and opportunities to find a job outside of prostitution. Brittany's role was to go into bars and clubs during the day to talk with the young girls about the organization and the opportunities available. It required bold action on Brittany's part and taught her something truly amazing.

Her preconceived notions about prostitution—the type of women involved, their morals, personalities, etc.—were completely dispelled. Instead of meeting disreputable women, as she expected, she met smart, hardworking women trapped in a terrible situation because of financial troubles.

She listened with compassion, as one after another told the story of how they had come to prostitution. It seemed that each story involved an "end of the rope" moment, the final straw that convinced them to accept prostitution as their only option.

Those "end of the rope" moments had stuck with Brittany. She couldn't stop thinking about what would be possible if an organization reached out to women during that bleakest moment to prevent them from going down a dark road.

It was a thought that stayed with her as she returned to the States to study International Relations at Michigan State. When she returned home, the first thing she did was buy a Thai language book—she knew that as soon as she graduated, she wanted to be back in Thailand.

After graduating from college, with $300 left in her bank account, she boarded a plane for Bangkok. She figured that would be enough money to survive for two months while she searched for a job with a non-profit or non-governmental organization in the area.

* * *

For a while Brittany, played around with the idea of starting her own business, but it was always more of a daydream than an actual desire. A few years before, her brother had bought her a tote bag crocheted with recycled plastic bags. She loved the uniqueness of the bag and often received compliments from people while she was wearing it.

Her brother was also doing humanitarian work in Thailand. He had fallen in love with the country when volunteering in a refugee camp after the tsunami in 2004. He knew how much Brittany liked the bag, and pointed out that it wouldn't be hard to make one herself—in fact, it might just be a great business opportunity for her.

Brittany liked the idea, and had fun brainstorming about how she would start a company, but that's as far as the idea went. Brittany didn't believe in herself enough to take the next step, to turn the idea into action. She wasn't crafty; she had never taken a business class. She simply didn't have the skills to make it happen. She also had school loans to pay off, which meant getting a job with a larger organization would be "the responsible thing to do."

So she ditched the idea and jumped into a job-search. But then, something happened. Her roommate, Panida, a Thai woman she met at Michigan State, came home with devastating news. Her supervisor had come to her in tears—she was struggling to make ends meet at her current job... and had decided to start prostituting.

She was at the end of her rope.

Brittany knew she had to do something. This was her chance to intervene before it was too late.

The idea of starting a company re-emerged. She still wasn't convinced it would work, but she decided to try. She bought the needed materials, found instructions online, and sewed (in her words) the world's ugliest little bag. But it was a completed bag, and it was a start.

Panida joined Brittany in her efforts. They approached her supervisor about the possibility of her working for their new company making bags.

The supervisor quickly said no.

Like Brittany, she didn't believe in herself. She didn't know how to make a bag, and she was afraid to try.

Brittany and Panida refused to give up. They told her they would leave her the supplies and instructions, and encouraged her to give it a shot. When they returned a week later, the supervisor opened the door with a big smile on her face. She held up a completed bag with pride in her eyes—she proved to herself she could do it.

Although it was also "one of the world's ugliest little bags," it was a start.

Sometimes, that's all you need.

With practice, they began making beautiful bags that they sold in the United States, United Kingdom and online through Brittany's company Thai Song. The company she thought would never work was approaching its second anniversary. And, more importantly, they employed six women who felt empowered, dignified, and confident.

* * *

At the ripe age of 24, Brittany Fox has already changed many lives. Perhaps that's why she felt so connected to Thailand when she first arrived: it needed help and, somewhere deep inside, Brittany knew she could provide it.

Cup 47 taught me the value of testing our assumptions, instead of simply assuming an idea won't work.

Brittany could have stuck to the belief that her idea wouldn't work.

But she didn't.

And now six women in Thailand are facing a much brighter future.

STEVE SCHRAM

Michigan Radio Headquarters in Ann Arbor, Michigan
Green tea

**Uncertainty is inevitable, but you don't have to
tackle it alone.**

I wasn't in the best of spirits the Monday I drove to Ann Arbor to meet Steve Schram. I had had one of those weekends where everything felt uncertain: I questioned every choice I was making, and I worried I was setting goals I wasn't fit to achieve.

In short, my confidence had faltered.

It happens to everyone. With 365 days in a year, you're bound to have a handful of bad ones. In fact, you're lucky if you only have a handful.

My focus over the past few weeks had been determining what would happen after my post-college travels came to an end. I wanted to continue traveling, but my dwindling bank account was a constant reminder that I had to find a way to make it financially feasible.

One of the greatest lessons I'd learned through 52 Cups was this: with the right combination of passion, courage, persistence, and elbow grease, anything could happen. That's why I was pursuing what I truly wanted in a career rather than settling on a 9-to-5 that didn't fit me. My pursuit had more uncertainty and risk than the typical job-route, but I could handle the uncertainty; I'd heard enough success stories to know the end result would be well worth the effort.

Okay, saying I could handle the uncertainty was not entirely true. A more accurate statement would be that I could handle the uncertainty 95 percent of the time. The weekend before Cup 48 fell into the five percent of the time when I worried I'd bitten off more than I could chew and was too naive to notice.

That's why I went to have coffee with Steve Schram.

The only thing I knew about Steve—aside from his job title of Director of Public Media at Michigan Radio—was that he was a close friend of one of my mentors, Scott Westerman. During a conversation with Scott, I told him I needed to have coffee with someone who gave good advice. Scott said Steve was the perfect person, so I set up a meeting and hit the road to Ann Arbor.

* * *

When I arrived at the Michigan Radio office in downtown Ann Arbor, Steve gave me a warm welcome before getting us both a cup of green tea from the break room. We began the conversation by exchanging stories about how we both knew Scott. I explained that I'd met him two years ago through my involvement with entrepreneurship at MSU.

Steve told me he'd met Scott over 30 years before, through his involvement with the campus radio at MSU. When Steve and Scott were in college, the campus radio scene was hot. This was back before iTunes, YouTube, and Spotify made music accessible with just a few clicks. Back then, if you wanted to hear the latest track you had to tune into the radio or call and request a song from the DJ.

Steve was one of those DJs, and he loved it. From a young age he knew he wanted to be in radio. During high school, he and a group of friends created a pirate-radio station that they programmed every day after school. They treated it just like a regular station and focused on making it as professional as possible. Joining campus radio at Michigan State was an obvious next step and one that led to a successful career in the radio industry. Steve told me he never needed to join a fraternity; his friends in campus radio were like family, and that remained true even after 30 years.

While I had very limited knowledge about radio, I understood Steve's experience. My "fraternity" in college was a group of entrepreneurs that were crazy enough to think they could each build a company of their own and excited to help others do the same.

When I told Steve this, he replied that I would end up being friends with many of those students for the rest of my life. We'd go to each others' weddings, celebrate career successes, and more. He continued to say that we wouldn't just celebrate great moments; we'd help each other through the tough times too.

A few years back, when Scott's daughter was getting married in Florida, Steve flew down to attend the wedding.

At the time, Scott had a great job but was a considering an opportunity at Michigan State. Steve could see the decision weighing heavily on Scott's mind, so during the reception he pulled Scott outside to talk. He listened to Scott's concerns before expressing his opinion that the job would be a perfect fit, something certainly worth pursuing. Steve wasn't trying to tell Scott what to do or make the decision for him, he just wanted to give an outside perspective and supportive voice.

Scott ultimately pursued the job and was now thriving at Michigan State.

Of course, Steve didn't take credit for Scott's decision. His advice was just one of the many factors involved. But it was an important piece, since Steve was a trusted friend and confidant.

I appreciated the story for a number of reasons. For starters, it was comforting to know that everyone—even those we most admire—struggles with moments of uncertainty. More importantly, it made me feel comfortable enough to open up and ask Steve for advice.

I told him about the goals I was trying to achieve, how I hoped to achieve them, and the uncertainties and concerns I had about the process. Although I had known him for less than 30 minutes, I knew I could trust him to give me encouraging, honest advice about my situation.

I was right. After listening to my story, Steve asked me questions about things I hadn't considered and made observations I hadn't noticed. Then he shared insights from his career experience and the experience he'd had raising two sons.

By the end of the conversation, the uncertainty of my situation wasn't quite so overwhelming. Steve helped me see the situation from an objective and practical perspective, rather than the emotional and speculative viewpoint I'd held all weekend. I realized that I had become so wrapped up in emotions about my future I wasn't able to think clearly. I needed someone to help me take a step back and see the situation from a higher level.

Scott had sent me to Steve because he knew Steve could help me do that.

* * *

Cup 48 is an important reminder that there will always be moments of uncertainty in life. But more importantly, there will also always be people who can help us through them—it is just a matter of being brave enough to seek out help and open up.

It is also a reminder that if you have an opportunity to help someone else, you should take it. Nobody can do it all by themselves.

STEVE GOOGIN

Greyrock Farms outside Syracuse, New York
Fresh cow milk

Many great ideas seem crazy—until they work.

Cup 49 did not involve any coffee. But it did include raw cow milk.

I bet you didn't see that one coming.

I didn't either.

It all began when a crazy idea infiltrated my mind while filling up my car before an eight-day road trip with my friend Rachel: *We should find a way to milk a cow!*

In all honesty, I have no idea why I had the idea. Luckily, I knew my travel companion Rachel would be game for the challenge. When I picked her up, I told her the idea, and we began brainstorming ways to make it happen. We weren't aware of any protocol for finding a cow to milk, so we resorted to telling any stranger we ran into about our idea, hoping we'd somehow find a lead to a dairy cow.

Our strategy worked. We met a wonderful young woman named Abigail through a travel service called Airbnb, which allows people to rent out space in their homes. We stayed at her barn-turned-renovated-home outside of Syracuse, New York. During our first night, we stayed up well past midnight, getting to know each other. At some point, we brought up our cow-milking quest and Abigail knew the perfect person to help us make it happen: Steve Googin, an acquaintance of hers who worked at an area farm.

She gave us his phone number; we exchanged a few text messages, and the next day Rachel and I were tromping around Greyrock Farm, learning about crops, cattle, and community-supported agriculture.

* * *

Community-supported agriculture (CSA) is a socioeconomic model of agriculture whereby individuals in the community pay a membership fee and in return receive a box of fresh produce each week throughout the farming season. The result is that CSA members get local produce picked at the peak of freshness while farmers have more financial stability and get to connect with the people who eat their food. CSAs have been around for years, but the model is growing in popularity.

Rachel and I were lucky to visit Greyrock on a pickup day, which meant while we toured the farm, carloads of individuals and families showed up to pick veggies from the neatly stacked bins inside one of the barns. Each person who walked into the barn received a warm welcome from Steve and the other farmers. It was clear that Greyrock was more than just a farm; it was a community of people who cared about each other.

I had never heard of CSAs, but after listening to Steve explain the details, and watching dozens of members leave with armloads of veggies and smiles on their faces, I loved the idea. It seemed like a desirable alternative to shopping for veggies under the fluorescent lights of an impersonal big-box store. The passion in Steve's voice as he told us the history of the

farm and his story only intensified our fascination for supporting local farming.

At one time, Greyrock was a dairy farm operated by two
women. When the women got older, they needed someone to
take over. That's when they found Matt Volz, a young farmer
looking to start a CSA. Matt convinced Steve, who was a
friend from high school, to join the crew; although the idea of
joining a small sustainable farm in the middle of nowhere
might have seemed a little crazy, Steve was easily convinced.
He was passionate about the idea and could see its potential to
positively impact the community.

* * *

After Steve had given us a tour of the farm, we got down to
business. Steve led the two dairy cows into the barn for their
afternoon milking as Rachel and I nervously followed. It was
clear that the cows were used to, and looked forward to, this
part of their afternoon. It was also clear that Rachel and I had
no idea what we were doing. Luckily. Steve was a great teacher and patiently walked us through the process.

It's difficult to accurately describe what it feels like to milk
a cow. I suppose "awkward" and "a little frustrating" are fitting
adjectives. Most of the milk ended up on the ground instead
of in the milk bucket, but it was a fun experience nonetheless.
It was certainly not an experience to pass up on if ever given
the chance.

After Rachel and I both had a chance to try, Steve took
over and, once both cows were milked, offered us a taste of
raw milk from the morning's milking. I figured it was an
acceptable substitute for a cup of coffee—and also a fitting

way to celebrate accomplishing our strange quest to milk a cow.

* * *

Is milking a cow a spectacular accomplishment? Not really. Many people do it every day.

But what was a cause for celebration was the fact that we turned a crazy idea into a reality. What we were celebrating was a mentality, a pursuit.

Two mentalities, really: our attempt to accomplish a challenge and Greyrock's attempt to innovate a better food system in its community.

What had begun as something nonsensical had turned into a valuable experience: a lesson in the importance of understanding where food comes from and its ability to build community and nourish the spirit as well as the body. When we left the farm, we had armfuls of fresh veggies and some new friends. We also took away great memories and new knowledge.

That wouldn't have happened if we had dismissed the crazy idea before giving it a chance. It wouldn't have happened if we hadn't accepted the challenge and followed our curiosity.

The more I thought about Cup 49, the harder it was to keep the words of Apple CEO Steve Jobs out of my head. I had heard his Stanford commencement speech a few years earlier, but watched it again after his passing, which happened a few weeks before visiting the farm. Within the speech was a quote that I often repeat to myself: *Your time is limited; so don't waste it living someone else's life.*

Jobs continued, "Don't be trapped by dogma—which is living with the results of other people's thinking. Don't let the noise of others' opinions drown out your own inner voice. And most importantly, have the courage to follow your heart and intuition. They somehow already know what you truly want to become. Everything else is secondary."

Cup 49 was an adventure, a new experience, and, most importantly, a reminder to chase crazy dreams. Because most great ideas seem crazy—until they work.

CLARK BUNTING

Discovery Channel Headquarters in Silver Spring, Maryland
Medium house coffee

The way you get from Point A to Point B won't be a straight line. That's okay.

When I met Clark Bunting, he was the president and general manager of *Discovery Channel*. For the past 25 years, he had been a part of the team that brought to life programs like *Planet Earth*, *Shark Week*, and *Deadliest Catch*.

He was also a proud Michigan State Spartan, so I reached out to him to see if he'd meet me for coffee while I was in Washington, D.C. on a road trip.

He said yes, and a few weeks later, I was at the Discovery Headquarters in Silver Spring, Maryland outside of D.C. When I walked into the lobby, I found a massive dinosaur skeleton, photo-lined walls featuring network celebrities, and a great assortment of memorabilia from *Discovery* shows.

After I went through security, Clark's assistant, Laurie, met me in the lobby. We took the elevator up to Clark's floor, and I waited for him in a small conference room where a picture of *Dirty Jobs* star Mike Rowe covered in mud stared at me. Clark walked in and introduced himself before we jumped into a conversation that continued as we took the elevator down to the coffee shop on the first floor.

Clark was often called "the guy who started *Shark Week*," so I couldn't resist asking him how he felt about being known for the TV event with a cult following. He humbly pointed out that it had been a team effort before sharing a few amusing stories from the production. Stories that ranged from working with actor Andy Samburg to orchestrating live video shoots of sharks feeding in the middle of the ocean: it was obvious that Clark's career had been out-of-the-ordinary.

* * *

Clark's original plan had been a career on Capitol Hill. After receiving a Master's degree from Michigan State, he and his wife had moved to Washington, D.C. where he got a job as a legislative assistant. It was during this job that he realized politics might not be the route for him. He looked at many of the lifestyles of the people who had been on the Hill for years: perpetually stressed and overworked, a high number of failed marriages, and problems with substance abuse. It wasn't the lifestyle he wanted, so he decided to look for a job elsewhere.

The job he found was with a young company called Cable Educational Network. He met with the founder, John Hendricks, and realized they shared a similar vision and entrepreneurial spirit. At the time, a big void existed in television programming—there were news, sports, and entertainment channels, but nothing educational. Cable Educational Network set out to change that. The company, which grew rapidly, eventually changed their name to Discovery Channel and became the most widely distributed channel in the world.

Clark, as one of the original employees, played a pivotal role in the company's growth. He helped bring many of Discovery's popular programs to life before taking over as president in 2010. It was a role that he took very seriously. He knew the shows Discovery produced were having an impact on millions of viewers around the world—he was also having a lot of fun.

At one point in his career, he was dangling a dead chicken over a hungry croc, while Steve Irwin coached him through the feeding process (certainly nothing he had expected when he responded to the classified ad). Clark said moments like that make you pause and think: *How did I get myself into this position?*

The answer to that question was a bit of luck, mixed with creativity, passion and a lot of hard work. Most importantly, he found meaning in the work. Discovery Channel uses the power of entertainment to shine light on important issues. Clark used Steve Irwin as an example. The two became close friends when Clark helped create and produce *The Crocodile Hunter*. The show, which became wildly popular, served a greater role than just entertainment. Clark said Steve's genius was his ability to get people to care. He wasn't just a crazy Aussie playing with reptiles; he was a passionate environmentalist who helped people see the world from a new perspective and generate positive environmental change.

Clark explained that Discovery succeeded because two things held true for people: they are naturally curious, and they love to hear a good story. *The Crocodile Hunter* wasn't the only show that told intriguing stories that served a greater purpose. *Planet Earth* was a remarkable series that let people gain a new appreciation and concern for the environment; *Shark Week* helped pass a law to ban shark finning; and shows like *Mythbusters* had gotten viewers excited about science.

As I listened to Clark talk, I was fascinated by the realization that he ultimately achieved the goal he was pursuing on Capitol Hill, he just had to leave the Hill to do it. His goal was to affect laws and generate positive change. While he thought politics would be the way to do that, he discovered that, for him, entertainment was the solution. It reminded me of something author Randy Pausch said in his famous Last Lecture: *It's not about how to achieve your dreams; it's about how to lead your life. If you lead your life the right way, the karma will take care of itself; the dreams will come to you.*

Clark lived his life around a certain moral foundation: he wanted to lead a good life for himself and his family, and he wanted to do work that mattered. It may have been a stroke of luck that he stumbled into a great opportunity, but luck wouldn't make you the president of a major company—Clark had worked hard to make Discovery Channel something fantastic. He has led his life with integrity, and the result has been an incredible career that has changed lives as well as the planet.

The most valuable lesson I took from Cup 50 is that the way you get from Point A (the start of a career) to Point B (the end) isn't going to be a straight line. But if you keep moving toward a goal you're shooting for, you'll get there.

Probably not in the way you expect.

Or in the time frame you think.

But if you persevere and live right, you'll get there, and hopefully have fun in the process.

ELAINE ROSENBLATT

When life changes unexpectedly, grieve, grow, and move forward.

I'll be honest; Cup 51 was hard to write.

There are a lot of explanations for why, but I think the most-relevant one is that I didn't want the project to end—because I didn't know what came next. The irony was that this Cup is about learning to let go and moving on to something better.

* * *

I met with Elaine Rosenblatt on a windy and gloomy Wednesday. I took the train to the outskirts of Chicago and arrived at the Starbucks first. When Elaine walked in, I recognized her immediately. She looked just like her son Brett, the stranger who had invited me to coffee three years ago, became one of my best friends, and showed me the power of reaching out to people you don't know.

Elaine lived outside of Chicago, and when I was invited to attend a fundraiser in Chicago, I decided to reach out to her to see if she could meet while I was in town. I thought it was fitting that she could help me end a project that her son had helped me start. I had also heard enough about her from Brett that I was certain she could give me good advice.

I caught Elaine's attention and introduced myself before we stood in line to get coffee. Because of her warm and nurturing spirit and the fact that we had a lot in common, we were already deep in conversation by the time we sat down at a small table by the window.

I had a feeling the conversation was going to go in all different directions, so I asked my most-important question first: "How did you end up where you are today?" I didn't know anything about Elaine other than that she was a psychotherapist and had three sons.

It started out as a very simple story. For as long as she could remember, the only thing Elaine wanted to be when she grew up was a mom. She hadn't considered college or a career. She'd fallen in love, gotten married, and had a son in her early twenties. She had achieved her goal.

Of course, that was not where the story ends. It's where it began.

Elaine's marriage began to crumble, and before she knew it, she found herself a single mom with a child to support. Desperate for work, she took the first job she could find: a job at a clinic for women, where she unexpectedly discovered a love for advocacy work.

As her involvement in her job increased, she gained national attention for her work, becoming a sought-after voice for women's sexual rights, often doing radio interviews and speeches on the topic. Although she hadn't followed the traditional educational route, she was passionate and constantly worked to stay educated about her field while preparing for the next step.

In the process of building her career, she remarried and had two more kids (the youngest was Brett). She said that even with all of her career success, raising her three boys was her life's greatest joy. Being a mom was a perfect fit for her nurturing spirit. It also helped her realize she had a natural ability to counsel others and help them through their problems. While engaged in advocacy work she started taking classes to become a certified divorce mediator, and then later a psychotherapist.

Elaine was a strong, independent, complex and compassionate woman. Having coffee with her reminded me so much of the first conversation I ever had with Brett—the conversation just clicked.

When I asked her how people get through a difficult divorce, her response was straightforward: "You just do." Her son depended on her; she had no choice but to find a way to get through the hardship.

That's how our conversation took a deep dive into the nature of pain and hardships—two inevitable parts of life. While that may seem like a somber topic, the conversation was very encouraging.

It wasn't until Elaine tested her strength that she realized how strong she could be. It wasn't until she was forced to find work that she realized she could create an incredible career for herself. It was because she could navigate through her own pain that she discovered she could help others navigate through theirs. In short, the sadness in her life led her to a place of incredible happiness.

But it didn't happen overnight.

When she married her first husband, she expected to stay married to him forever and built her hopes and dreams around that scenario. It is something we probably all would do. We become attached to visions of the future—expected outcomes over which we have little control—until the illusion feels like reality.

Then something happens—the relationship falls apart, the job isn't all that it's cracked up to be, the economy goes south—and the illusion (along with the feeling of security) shatters.

It is a story that happens to everyone at some point, and one Elaine frequently hears in her work. The advice she gives comes down to three steps: grieve, believe, and wait out the discomfort.

When a major life change happens, it is all right (and normal!) to be upset. Trying to cover up or numb the pain doesn't make it go away any faster. The best course of action is to embrace it and give yourself time to grieve.

But in the process of grieving, you shouldn't lose sight of the light at the end of the tunnel: faith, religion, optimism—call it what you want; it is hope for the future. If you can't find it in yourself, find someone who can help you find it. Like Brett told me a week earlier when I'd called him during a particularly bad day: "History repeats itself—if you survived tough times in the past, you've proven you can survive tough times in the future."

Then, once you find the hope, accept that there is going to be a period of discomfort. Elaine went back to the tunnel metaphor. You know there is a light at the end, but it is going to be dark and uncertain for a while. It is an uncomfortable place to be, but if you keep pushing forward, you can make it to the end, and be stronger as a result.

* * *

While Elaine's advice centered on hardship, it was also a solution for any change. It was a process for saying goodbye to what had been, and looking forward to what will be.

52 Cups had been a big part of my life for the last year. Now I had to prepare for a post-52 Cups life. Leaving the security of this project for the unknown of the next one was a little uncomfortable. Coffee with Elaine reminded me that 52 Cups had prepared me for whatever's next. While closing this chapter of my life would be difficult, I had learned to embrace change and use my experiences to make my next chapters even better.

CUP 52

Boogaloos in San Francisco, California
Small brewed coffee

**Figure out what you love, then find the courage to
do it, and do it well.**

It's Tuesday morning, and I'm sitting at an adorable breakfast spot in San Francisco, eating some of the best bacon and eggs I've ever had, and enjoying a cup of coffee that the waitress will refill at least three times before I leave.

All through my senior year, people asked me where I'd be after graduation. I assumed I would be in a cubicle somewhere, climbing the corporate ladder on the fast track to a promotion and increasingly impressive job titles and salaries. That's what you're supposed to do with an expensive college degree, right?

And, if I hadn't decided to do this crazy experiment in caffeine and conversation, it's probably what I would be doing; I called 52 Cups of Coffee an experiment, as I knew meeting 52 new people would inevitably change my life. I just didn't know how.

I can tell you I didn't expect it would inspire me to trade the job-search for six months spent traveling to 15 different countries where each day I woke up excited about the uncertainty of where that day would lead.

During my senior year, the uncertainty of my future after graduation created a crippling fear. My mindset was that I had one shot to figure out my life. The day after graduation was the first day of the rest of my life, and if I didn't have the perfect plan in place (and the perfect job), I would be setting myself up for irreconcilable failure.

Where that thought came from, I don't know, but I know it was a real fear. I also know I am incredibly grateful for those who had coffee with me and helped me understand the irrationality in my thinking.

It started during the first ten Cups when I realized a very noticeable trend: nobody's life had gone according to plan. Life throws a lot of curveballs. Sometimes they're good ones: unexpectedly falling in love, discovering a passion, stumbling into an incredible career opportunity. And sometimes they test your strength: losing a loved one, experiencing a breakup, going through a layoff or unexpected illness.

Understanding that life won't go according to plan leaves you with two choices: let the fear of the unknown overwhelm you, or embrace the uncertainty.

I'll tell you from experience that the former is easier than the latter, for two reasons:

First, it takes a lot of faith (and confidence) to embrace uncertainty and believe you can handle whatever life throws your way. I only found faith because I had these conversations with people from various backgrounds; each reaffirming that life always works out if you've got the right approach.

The second reason is that believing in yourself is only half the battle. The second half is execution. If you are open to go where life takes you, you can end up in incredible places. But you can't just sit back and expect a great life, you have to go out and make one.

The magic of sitting down with strangers—putting yourself in a vulnerable position and taking time to genuinely listen to their stories—is that you can put a story behind the advice. The advice becomes real, and it becomes personal. I have a catalog of anecdotes I now carry with me.

On days filled with obstacles, I think about Cup 17, Piotr Pasik, traveling to Europe and playing indoor soccer, despite having limited mobility due to cerebral palsy. When my dreams feel too big, I think about Cup 36, Tom Izzo, a graduate assistant for the MSU basketball team making a $4,000 salary at age 30, dreaming about one day becoming head coach.

When I think about what I want in a career, I think about Cup 21, Torya Blanchard, and what she calls her "Fight Club moment"—the instant she decided she was going to quit her job and cash in her 401K to start a (now-thriving) restaurant in Detroit. Then, when the fear of failure starts to sink in, I hear Cup 38, Seth Godin, saying, "You're not failing enough. I failed countless times before I was 30—and that's what led to my success."

The words of Cup 13, Dave Isbell, echo the importance of staying humble, while Cup 5, Dave Murray, reminds me that life is about more than creating a great life for yourself, it's about giving back and creating a great life for others as well. Encountering a vibrant six-year-old evokes memories of my conversation with Cup 22, Abby Ward, an adopted Native American girl in a town without much diversity, who taught me that everyone has an interesting story, but too often we make assumptions instead of asking questions.

When I hear of tragedies, I think of Cup 25, Betsy Miner-Swartz, losing both of her parents to cancer in a short time and how she used the love and support of family and friends to make it through the pain, one step at a time. Then I ask myself, *when was the last time I told my loved ones how important they are to me?*

This is just the tip of the iceberg. Every Cup has changed me. The best way to describe the change is a quote from Cup 51, Elaine Rosenblatt: "People need to learn to stop looking at life from the outside in and start looking from the inside out."

When I started 52 Cups, I was obsessed with living up to other people's expectations, with becoming the person others wanted me to be. Over the course of this project, I realized this is no way to live life. I have to look inside and figure out who I am, then decide where I want to fit in the rest of the world.

That's why I decided to travel.

I followed my love for travel and hoped it would lead me to the next step. And it did. When I stopped looking for the perfect job and focused on what I loved, the perfect job found me. Michigan State's Alumni Association offered me a six-month position, where I would visit various cities to connect with young alumni—a great position for a traveler with a love for good conversation.

And what will happen once that job is over?

I don't know.

But that's okay.

Because I know that if I can continue to figure out what I love to do, find the courage to do it, and do it well, life will work out, and I'll have a lot of fun in the process.

When I set out to meet 52 new people, I didn't realize that the most important person I would meet was the person I became.

ACKNOWLEDGMENTS

This book project has been a group effort from the start. It would not exist without the 52 wonderful people that graciously shared their story with me, and allowed me to share it with others. Thank you for your time, your insights and, in many cases, your friendships; they have had a lasting effect on me.

52 Cups of Coffee project had a strong start thanks to Brett Kopf, who invited me to coffee and became a great friend (we both owe Kelley Bishop a big thank you for putting us in touch); Jeff Grabill, who helped me find my voice; and Scott Westerman, who believed in the project from day one—he also made the best introductions.

You're holding this book because of the incredible help of Kevin Liu for organizing the pages and keeping me on track and Rachel Balanon for the cover. Andrew Vilcsak, Gail Lasham, and my parents Jane and Gregg Gebhart. I don't think my dad knew what he was getting into when he volunteered to be my editor—but I'm sure grateful he did.

I was lucky to have girlfriends like Jennifer Yee, Jeannine Seidl, Rachel Balanon, Hillary Welton, Jessica Colombo, and Kelly Steffen during the adventure. Thank you for being editors, road trip companions, confidants, generous hosts during my nomadic year, and so much more.

I uncovered many of these wonderful stories thanks to the help of friends that generously made introductions for me or provided support along the way. Thank you for your help Andrew and Sandy Gebhart, Peg Ostlund, Eric Jorgensen, Jake Lestan, Henry Balanon, Avish Bhama, John Hill, Todd

Ross, Bill Ward, Payal Ravani, Spencer Nordwick, Richard Ward, Emily Winter, Robin Miner-Swartz, Amanda VanderMeulen, Kelly Bennett, Christine Garland, Jim Cotter, Piotr Pasik, Kim Gebhart, Vivian Leung, and Abigail Henson.

This is a non-exhaustive list. There are countless family members, friends and readers that liked, shared, and commented on the original blog posts. Those positive words of encouragement were invaluable and kept me motivated to keep writing.

Thank you.

ABOUT THE AUTHOR

Megan Gebhart is a storyteller, speaker, and writer. Originally from Wyoming, Megan attended Michigan State University, where she immersed herself in a community of daring entrepreneurs and began entrepreneurial ventures of her own.

In 2010 Megan created 52 Cups of Coffee, a website dedicated to the power of connection. What started as an experiment to have coffee with a stranger every week for a year turned into a global exploration filled with serendipity and stories that teach us that finding ourselves is a journey that can last a lifetime.

Today, Megan continues to meet and profile inspiring people. She shares their stories and lessons at conferences and colleges throughout the United States to inspire others to reach out and connect with new people over coffee.

You can tell Megan about your own cups of coffee on Twitter @megangebhart or over email at megan@52cups.com

CPSIA information can be obtained
at www.ICGtesting.com
Printed in the USA
LVHW112312120719
624002LV00001B/5/P